A CHARGE TO KEEP

METHODIST REFLECTIONS ON THE EVE OF THE THIRD MILLENNIUM

Compiled by Brian Thornton

ISBN 1 85852 139 4

© 1999 Trustees for Methodist Church Purposes

All rights reserved. No part of this publication may be produced, stored in a retrieval system, transmitted, in any form or by any means, electronic, mechanical, photocopying, recording or otherwise, without the prior permission of the publishers Methodist Publishing House, 20 Ivatt Way, Peterborough PE3 7PG

Scripture quotations, unless otherwise stated, are from the New Revised Standard Version of the Bible, copyright 1989 by the Division of Christian Education of the National Council of the Churches of Christ in the USA.

CONTENTS

Foreword
Nigel Collinson   1

Spirituality
Stuart Burgess   3

Stop the Church –
I want others to get on
Heather Cooper   10

From College to Conference
The reflections of a probationer
Steve Mann   17

Ring of Faith: The Circuit
Margaret Woodlock-Smith   24

Rural, Relevant and Realistic
John Clarke   31

The Suburban Church
Andrew Foster   38

In the City, Out of Love
John Lampard   45

No Mid-Life Crisis Here!
A view from the middle years
Mary Bailey   52

No Banana Republic
A District View
Eddie Lacy   57

Wearing Well!
>	*Michael Hayman* 61

More than Words?
>	Christian Apologetics for a New Millennium
>	*Martyn Atkins* 68

Developing Partnerships –
>	Meeting you where you are
>	*Caro Ayres* 76

International and Interdependent
>	*Kathleen Richardson* 83

Elders Not Oldies
>	*Albert Jewell* 90

'It's of Little Concern'
>	*Bill Lynn* 96

Faith in Ourselves
>	*Brian Thornton* 104

Contributors   110

FOREWORD

This book is about the task and the vision committed to the Methodist Church. At a time when the talk is about cutbacks and decline, it says that there is still much to do, and there are the resources to do it, if only we will have confidence in God and in ourselves.

That is a theme which I have returned to constantly during my ministry. Ever since I became a Methodist minister people have been telling me that things ain't what they used to be. It's almost as though we treasured the past more than the present moment. Of course, it's tough now, I grant you. There are many places where we are just about hanging on. Sometimes, however, that hanging on is a sign of spiritual tenacity. When times are hard, just being there is enough.

Equally there are places which are being renewed by the vision of people and pastor and the grace of God working through them. I was present at an Easter Day service this year when 24 young people became members of the Methodist Church. But the constantly renewing presence of God does not always mean huge numbers of people, good though that is. There are many quite modest Methodist churches which have discovered their vocation in the community under God and have become effective.

What matters is that we recognise the distinctive marks of the Methodist Church, not in a triumphalist fashion – the time for that is long gone – but in a humble, thankful way. *A Charge to Keep* is about what is distinctively Methodist: a personal faith, a commitment to the local, a burning desire to see right prevail, an emphasis on caring for people, a belief in the word of the Gospel to give hope, peace and challenge. All these you will find in the essays which follow.

What you will not actually find written about in these pages, but which each writer communicates none the less, is passion, the belief that all this really matters. That is after all what you find in Charles Wesley's hymn, the first line of which lends itself as the title for the book. For him it was a matter of life and death. The Great Commission of Jesus to his followers was to make a difference in people's lives and faith, and as Methodism has learned it, it is a passionate affair. Just go back to one of our foundation documents, the Deed of Union, with which I seem to live daily at the moment. There you find what our purpose is. 'It ever remembers that in the providence of God Methodism was raised up to spread scriptural holiness through the land.' That's dynamic, inspirational, full of passion. There is an urgency about it.

We need to understand that soon, for a growing generation of young people, the twentieth century will seem as far away as did the Victorian era to those of us who were its children. They will have choices to make that are beyond our imagining, yet they will still be challenged by the age-old scourges of war, poverty and ignorance. Will Christianity make a difference in their world? And will the Methodist way, first conceived in a pre-modern world, continue to make a distinctive contribution? With the contributors to *A Charge to Keep*, I believe it can if we have a passionate belief in the central things of the Gospel.

Nigel Collinson

SPIRITUALITY

The word 'spirituality' is perhaps an overused one today, and its meaning has widened from the earlier 'devotional life' or Bishop Jeremy Taylor's 'the rule and exercise of holy living'. There seems to be a hunger amongst people who want a spiritual dimension in their lives but who do not really know what they are looking for, or where to find it if they did. But they do feel a distaste for the all-encompassing materialism of Western life, and a sense that a prosperous lifestyle ruled by possessions is no longer enough. Their search for new meaning is not limited to Christianity, and some are exploring New Age beliefs, or the other world religions. Indeed it is important to recognise that all major faiths have their own spiritualities.

In the Christian Church there has been a move to recover a simpler yet more vivid awareness of God's presence in both worship and in daily Christian life. Christians are looking for greater spiritual growth, and for a deeper relationship with God, and they do not always find it in the traditional structures of the Church. On retreats and quiet days people are seeking God, often in silence and in a cessation of the constant activity which marks every aspect of our lives. In my opinion the concept of spirituality should be applied to the whole of life; it is not just about worship, or prayer, or about observing various spiritual disciplines, but about the way we live out our faith, in obedience, every day. We are called to be perfect, as our Father God is perfect (Matthew 5:48).

The Bible helps us to define the meaning of spirituality in our daily lives. The story of Mary and Martha (Luke 10:38-42), when Jesus and the disciples visited their home, is a good example of the need to find a balance between 'doing' and 'being'. Of course Martha wanted to make her guests welcome and give them the best meal she could, and in the same way we feel that we have to be busy doing God's work all the time, taking on more and more commitments. Instead, like Mary, we should be sitting at Jesus' feet, listening to what he has to say to us, before we start doing what he would have us do.

Some people feel that this waiting in quietness on God is an attempt to rediscover the 'numinous', that awe-inspiring feeling of the supernatural in our own world, a fleeting moment when we feel a heightened awareness of God's presence. To some, this is especially apparent in nature. The poet Richard Realf writes:

> All shapes and sounds have something
>   which is not
> Of them; a Spirit broods amid the grass;
> Vague outlines of the Everlasting Thought
>   Lie in the melting shadows as they pass;
> The touch of an Eternal Presence thrills
> The fringes of the sunsets and the hills.

In the Bible, Jacob had a more direct experience of the numinous in his dream of a ladder stretching up to heaven, leading him on waking to exclaim:

> *Surely the Lord is in this place – and I did not know it! . . . This is none other than the house of God, and this is the gate of heaven.*
>
> Genesis 28:16-17

Our search for a greater understanding of spirituality is helped by looking at the way in which people, in other times and in other ways, have searched for and found God. Nor should we look only at our own traditions; other faiths have much to teach us. I felt privileged once, on a visit to Nepal, to talk with a group of women about their Hindu faith and what it meant to them.

The spirituality of the Russian and Greek Orthodox Churches, for example, is rooted in the belief that the separation between God and his children has been abolished by the Incarnate Word. The Bible is of fundamental importance, and the Gospels are venerated as an icon of the living Word among the people of God. The icon is an integral part of Orthodox worship, and in recent years there has been a renewed interest among the Western Churches in icons and their purpose. In the Orthodox tradition worshippers stand or kneel in silence before an icon, or light a candle. The icon itself is not worshipped, but through it the worshipper seeks communion with God and his saints, and the icon is seen as an instrument through which God blesses the user.

One of the most important collections of icons is housed in St Catherine's monastery at the foot of Mount Sinai. Monastic life began there in the third century AD. Many Christians came to the desert lands of the Holy Land, Egypt and Syria, looking for a life of solitude and prayer, and living initially as hermits. In 305 an Egyptian named Antony began his life as a hermit in a mountain cave; eventually others came to seek his help and guidance. Communities such as St Catherine's began to appear; their members were known as 'cenobites', from the Greek, 'common life', and community buildings were called 'monasteries'.

The people who formed these first communities went to the desert to seek God in quietness and prayer, away from the crowded busyness and corruption of their world. They still had temptations to face; problems did not disappear, and neither they nor other people became saints overnight. Spirituality, wherever it is lived, is not meant to be only for one's own good. I remember a conversation I had with one of today's monks from St Catherine's who told me of his own struggle: 'It is here in the desert,' he said, 'that the starkness of life is to be seen. The desert experience focuses the mind and one is able to sort out the real priorities of living. It is not just an experience of extreme temperatures, but of coming to terms with oneself, with others and with God.'

The Celtic Church was greatly influenced by the desert experience, especially by its monastic way of life. Celtic spirituality attracts many people today. Its awareness of God in the everyday, ordinary events of life, its reverence for creation, and its emphasis on the 'immanence', or intense sense of the presence of God appeal to people who do not always find such things in the structures of the Church. Places such as Iona and Holy Island, where Christianity first took root in the British Isles, have become places of pilgrimage for people who are trying to incorporate Celtic spirituality into their own lives.

Both the desert monks and the Celtic saints, who sought out the lonely places of the world in order to pray and listen to what God was asking of them, put great stress on the silence of contemplation, on praying in solitude. Similarly, George Fox, the founder of the Quaker movement, believed that every person had an 'inner life' which could be received from God, leading to the 'light of life' and spiritual truth. Quaker meetings were, and are, held mainly in silence, allowing God to speak directly to the heart of each person, guiding and quickening them for service. In her book, *Worship* (Eagle 1991), Evelyn Underhill describes this silence: 'Quaker silence goes behind all expressive worship to that which inspires it, and makes direct metaphysical claim to communion with God in the inner deeps.'

In many churches today silence is a rare experience yet the spiritual life flourishes when silence becomes a part of it. It is a fundamental part of the Taizé 'experience', which greatly influenced my own spiritual growth. In what St Benedict called 'absolute silence' meditation and contemplation take over, and we enter the essence of prayer, not presenting God with a list of requests, but waiting on him, learning to listen to him.

African spirituality, on the other hand, emphasises joy in its worship, particularly expressed in dance, and I shall always remember the exuberant worship which I attended during a visit to Zambia. The other, quieter emphasis of African spirituality is that God is present in people's poverty. One of my most humbling and challenging experiences was an encounter with people in a bush community in Malawi. I saw poverty and little education, but I was aware of a deep spirituality as I listened and learned as people talked about their experience of God.

What of our own, Methodist, spirituality? John Wesley was greatly influenced by Bishop Jeremy Taylor's *Holy Living and Dying*, and Thomas à Kempis' *Imitation of Christ*, and he developed his own call to holiness, or search for Christian perfection, which he felt every person could be engaged in. This was not something that was easily attainable, nor did Wesley ever claim that he had reached it, but the working towards it was something everybody could try. By the work of the Holy Spirit, he said, a person's sin is gradually purged away, until that person loves God completely, and God 'is the joy of his heart, and the desire of his soul'. Wesley saw, like others before him, that spirituality is something that must touch all parts of our lives, must influence everything that we are and do:

> It is the giving God all our hearts; it is one desire and design ruling all our tempers. It is the devoting, not a part, but all, our soul, body and substance to God. In another view, it is all the mind which was in Christ, enabling us to walk as Christ walked.

This spirituality was to be worked out among others, helping and encouraging them on their own journeys of faith. Among the early Methodist people this was developed through the Class system, through Lovefeasts, through the challenge of the annual Covenant service and through the hymns of Charles Wesley and others.

Perhaps more important was Wesley's passion for the social gospel. Spirituality was no good if it was kept to oneself, or within a group of like-minded people; Methodist spirituality was to be found at work especially among the poor and sick, 'walking as Christ walked' among the downtrodden and weak. Personal holiness was to be allied with social responsibility to tackle the problems of the Victorian age. People such as Rev Hugh Price Hughes (1847-1902) fought to combine the evangelism of the Gospel with the provision of social welfare and education to combat the evils of exploitation, poverty and drunkenness, pioneering the work of the West London Mission.

What does the future hold for our own spirituality, in our complex society on the eve of the 21st century? The challenge is the same for us as it has been for others: we must find a way of linking a personal spirituality with obedience and action. When we have listened in silence to what God has to say to us we must take his love into the world in faith, prepared to get involved with the problems and issues which confront us. We need to draw on God's strength to help us to fight the evils of injustice through campaigns like Jubilee 2000; to care for God's world through environmental concerns; to be committed to peace; to be tolerant and to learn humbly from others. Above all we need to rediscover a sense of God, a sense of the numinous in our everyday lives, to gather at his table with others to be nourished, and then to face the challenges and opportunities which he gives us.

Stuart Burgess

STOP THE CHURCH – I WANT OTHERS TO GET ON

Methodism has a proud history. It was born to be a mission movement at a time when society was changing rapidly. The Industrial Revolution was transforming the largely agrarian society into an urban society, and in the face of such change the Church of England was failing to meet the needs of many people.

John and Charles Wesley experienced the transforming touch of God in their own lives and were inspired by a vision of what God could do and wanted to do in the nation. That vision led to the birth of Methodism, a movement for renewal, mission and the spread of scriptural holiness throughout the land. But today we seem, somehow, to have lost that strong sense of purpose.

Perhaps it was inevitable that, as the first generation of Methodists died, the vision died a little too. The following generations gradually replaced the dynamism of the early years with traditions and structures and expectations of what the Church should be like. However, that spark has always remained, a 'remnant' of men and women who know the power of God and who want to share the vision of what God can do in our nation today.

This has given us, I believe, a Church in transition. There are those who are holding on to the past like a security blanket, finding a stability in the familiarity of the Church which they have lost in our fast-changing society, while others see the need to change in response to the needs of our age so that the Church is no longer an alien place to people. We as a Church, not just the ministry, are trying hard to hold these different aspirations and longings together as we do not want to hurt or to lose anyone.

This, then, raises a question: do we *really* want others to join the Church? If not, we can carry on as we are, but if our answer is 'yes' then it is time to call a halt. Like a supertanker it could take a long time to stop, but if Methodism is to have any future it is time to stop and reassess who we are and what we are as a Christian community.

WHO ARE WE? WHAT ARE WE?

Our identity lies in our calling to be the people of God, the people called to fulfil the Great Commission:

> And Jesus came and said to them, 'All authority in heaven and on earth has been given to me. Go therefore and make disciples of all nations, baptising them in the name of the Father and of the Son and of the Holy Spirit, and teaching them to obey everything that I have commanded you. And remember, I am with you always, to the end of the age.
>
> Matthew 28:18-20

In these familiar words is a reminder that we are called to be faithful to the past, to the Gospel that we have inherited and are committed to passing on to those who come after us. It is a challenging call as we follow in the path of Jesus who often upset the establishment of his day with his words and actions.

The Great Commission reminds us that we are called to be faithful in passing on the teachings of Christ. This is not an excuse to abandon or ignore biblical scholarship or personal study any more than it is permission to reinterpret some of the less comfortable teachings of scripture. It is a call to obedience to the way of Christ, but how can we know the way of Christ if we do not place worship, prayer, the Bible and learning high on the list of our priorities?

The Bible Society has produced statistics about the reading of the Bible in our age which reveal that this best selling book is the least read, even among practising Christians. One of the problems facing Methodists, and indeed the whole Church, is a basic ignorance of Christianity amongst Christians themselves and it is this we need to address if we want others to share our faith.

So then, let's stop some of the frantic activity of our Church life to give us time to get in touch again with our faith. In the hymn 'Go forth and tell' are the words:

> How shall they call if they have never heard
> The gracious invitation of his word?
>
> HP 770

How can we tell others about God and Christ and the Holy Spirit if we, as Christians, remain unsure of our own faith?

It is when we are confident in our knowledge of our faith, imperfect as that knowledge will always be, that we will find a new ability to enjoy the rich heritage of our past without needing to cling on to that past as if it were a life raft. We will be able to build on the past, looking to the future because our knowledge of the Word will give us the security of who we are: the Body of Christ, the people of God, called to pass on the Good News.

WHO ARE WE TRYING TO REACH?

There is another reason to stop and reassess our situation; we need to understand our society. Sometimes it seems as if some Christians live in two separate worlds, the Church and the 'outside' world. But if we want people to get on with us we need to stop and take time to understand how our faith relates to our society.

There is a strong sense of alienation amongst many people, not just from the Church but also from neighbours, from creation, from political and economic systems and from the world of work. The fragmentation of our society has led to a sense of loss, lack of self-esteem and control over their own lives.

For a long time selfishness has been indulged in a society which has put personal happiness and the search for life before death above responsibility, and the price has been a loss of spiritual depth.

The result is that, as material values have been shown to be increasingly hollow and the much sought-after and vaunted 'feel-good' factor has proved to be an illusion, a spiritual hunger has grown. The tragedy is that in the search for spiritual meaning people do not think that the Church has anything to offer.

This is why we need to stop – to take time to rethink the way we respond to the society in which we live day by day and to remember that Church and society are not separate.

HOW DO WE RESPOND?

If we are to stop and reassess our attitudes we must also be willing to accept that we may have to change and to be open to new ways of being the Church. It seems that we can be our own worst enemies when we are faced with the opportunity to reach out to new people.

One example of this is the development of the Alpha Course which is designed to introduce people to the basics of the Christian Faith. It is not supposed to be a complete course in Christianity, but is meant to give Christians a way of inviting non-Christian friends to find out what it is all about. It has been used very successfully, yet it has attracted a great deal of criticism from within the Church, from people who do not agree with Alpha's theology. But Alpha is just one of many initiatives. Charter 95 is another, though more Methodist-based, challenge. Some initiatives reach more people than others do, some are more effective at stimulating existing faith and motivating mission while others are best at reaching outwards to non-Christians.

It is true that we should not blindly accept everything without question or testing, but neither should we be so negative about ways which are different from our own. Let's stop and think about our attitude to the ways in which new believers come to faith and celebrate their coming.

We need to remember, too, that the responsibility for making disciples and enabling them to join the Church is one which is for all of us, not just the minister's, or the steward's, or the youth worker's, or the evangelist's. Within every congregation there is a wide range of contacts to be made and talents to be used. It is sheep who make new sheep, not the shepherd, and we should all be ready to seize all the opportunities that God gives us.

From my place in the ordained ministry I believe we need a greater freedom from the traditional expectations of circuit work. We need the freedom to reach out and make links within the community without pressure from the Church to meet its demands. Ministers and deacons need to encourage and support church members in accepting new ways. We also need to be prodded sometimes.

Lay people need to take seriously the meaning of the 'priesthood of all believers', and they should be encouraged to exercise their gifts where they can do so best, without being pressured to fill church posts. Together we need to recover the confidence to be apologists, not apologetic about our faith, so that our evangelism is effective.

I believe that God called Methodism into being for a purpose. We have a rich heritage and a place within the great history of the Christian Church. I have great confidence in the future of God's Church and long for Methodism to be part of it. I believe this is an exciting time to be a Christian as we look towards a new millennium.

The question I would ask of all Methodists is this. We are proud of our heritage, but are we willing to build on our past not only for today but for tomorrow as well? Let's take time to stop, to think, to pray and to embrace God's will for the people called Methodists in the 21st century.

Heather Cooper

FROM COLLEGE TO CONFERENCE
The reflections of a probationer

It was on 21st June 1998 that I was ordained into the itinerant ministry of the Methodist Church. Whilst many of the emotions of the day had been keenly anticipated in advance, there was one incident that was totally unexpected. It was mid-afternoon and we ordinands were sitting on the platform at one end of the grand hall in the Spa Complex at Scarborough. Conference delegates filled the floor. Family and friends were in the gallery. At the other end of the hall was a solid wall of glass looking out on to the sea. So it was that as we proceeded through the service of Reception into Full Connexion my eyes were fixed on this expanse of blue. And there in the midst of it suddenly appeared a pirate ship carrying tourists back and forth across the bay. It was a bizarre not to say surreal juxtapositioning of images. Once again God was proved to have a sense of humour.

It also reminded me, as I confirmed my calling to serve God through the Methodist Church, that I am committed to a God of the unexpected. We are guided by a Holy Spirit who blows where he will and not always where we might anticipate. That does not always feel comfortable. We crave a paint-by-numbers Church that will magically appear when we follow a few familiar instructions. The last thing that we want is to find that the picture on the box has changed while we have been painting. Yet that is our reality. We live in a rapidly changing world that constantly challenges us to re-evaluate our methods of communicating the Gospel. At the same time we have faith in a God who more often than not asks us to wield the paintbrush without seeing the big picture. Never is this more keenly felt than by probationers facing new and unknown challenges whilst seeking to remain faithful to their calling.

It was on a January morning in 1996 that I received the 'phone call that was to confirm the location of my ministry for the next few years. After two years training at Queens College in Birmingham, I was to be stationed for my first, probationary, appointment in the Higham Ferrers and Raunds Circuit. This is semi-rural Northamptonshire, drifting across county boundaries into Bedfordshire in one direction and Cambridgeshire in the other.

The five churches under my pastoral care are a typical mixture of village and small town. The largest of these is at Raunds itself which was once a centre of the Northamptonshire shoe trade. In its heyday the industry provided everybody with employment. Nonconformity suited the working nature of the town and for much of this century Methodism thrived and was able to supply a complete spiritual and social package – even down to tennis courts and ballroom dancing. It could also for four years boast Sir David Frost as a son of the manse! Now the factories are almost all gone and people look elsewhere for jobs. Increasingly we are becoming a dormitory town. Our challenge as a church is not unique. We have to balance the legacy of the past and the strong community spirit of our older members with the changing lifestyles of a post-modern society.

After about a year here I came to a point of realisation. I suspect it is one that comes to every probationer. I discovered that I really could fill a minister's shoes. I could conduct a funeral and bring solace to the bereaved family. I could send people off into married life with joy. I could baptise a baby without it bawling. I could keep the attention of a school full of kids. I could visit young and old alike and still be invited back. I could meet with the other local clergy and not feel an impostor. So the list might go on. In short I had proved myself successful at all of the tasks of a modern minister. Yet at the same moment I realised that I was in danger. I was in danger of becoming an entertainer fulfilling expected roles and keeping people happy, when what I really yearned for was their spiritual development.

This is also the challenge that we face as a Church. We live in an age that values entertainment far more highly than commitment. Ultimate comfort is seen as more important than ultimate truth. Here at Raunds we see 'floaters' more and more – people who take part in church activities on an infrequent basis. For some this is down to working patterns or family situations but for many it is a case of attending unless there is a more attractive option. In order to draw people in we must be welcoming and provide worship and activities that people can relate to, but we must never subjugate our spiritual responsibility to that of keeping people happy. If we do we will accelerate what is already happening. A church will become a collection of individuals rather than a community; a circuit will become a collection of churches rather than a missionary entity and almost any sense of connexionalism will be lost.

Raunds has also caused me to question what, if anything, is distinctive about the Methodism of today. In the town we have four churches – Roman Catholic,

Anglican, Methodist and a Community church affiliated to the Pioneer grouping of independent evangelical churches. We work well together ecumenically and one of the reasons for this seems to me to be that we are all very different. We each have distinctive ways of worship and being 'church' and thus any sense of competitiveness is minimalised.

How, though, does Methodism fit into this scheme of things? It is easy to place the other Protestant churches. The Anglican church is high. The Community church is low and charismatic. Time and time again I find myself describing Methodism as lying somewhere in between and therein lies the nub of my problem. So often in Methodism we define ourselves negatively by what we're not rather than by what we are. We lose sight of our positive distinctiveness. It's like some of the families who come to me for a 'Methodist' funeral. No-one's ever seen them in church; they've no idea about Methodist doctrine but they know that being Methodist means that an Anglican or Baptist funeral won't do – even though their 'Methodism' might only derive from the fact that mother went to Sunday school or great-uncle Stan used to go on the chapel outings! Well might we mock, but we need to take a more positive pride in the rich heritage of Methodism that we carry forward.

Many will have their own idea of the distinctive character of Methodism but let me throw in my own suggestion born of the experiences of the last three years. That is the concept of mutual accountability. It has been reinforced both from the present and from the past.

During my probationary period I have had to look back as well as forward. Every probationer is required to undertake some form of study and mine metamorphasised into a Ph.D focusing on the life and ministry of John Fletcher, vicar of Madeley from 1760 to 1785. Fletcher was one of the early Methodist pioneers alongside the Wesley brothers. For two years I have lived and breathed him and often wondered what he would make of the late twentieth century.

Spending time immersed in this early period of Methodist development inevitably brings one face to face with the structures assembled by John Wesley for the spiritual development of the Methodist people. To belong to a Methodist society one had to be 'serious about religion' and have a desire to 'flee from the wrath to come'. Membership necessarily entailed belonging to a weekly class meeting. Members were also encouraged to be part of other small groups on a voluntary basis – bands, select bands or, for those who had fallen away, the penitents' classes. They were urged to 'join with mutual care to fight our passage through; and kindly help each other on, till all receive the starry crown'. Accountability was double-sided. A strong pastoral vehicle was established but also a means of ensuring spiritual growth through mutual awareness.

Times change and organisations evolve. What started as a connexion of societies within the Anglican Church became a Church in its own right. As this evolution took place the discipline that was possible within a society context became more difficult. The intense scrutiny that Wesley envisaged came to be seen as unnecessarily intrusive. Of the small groups only the class meeting survived and in most places today it survives in name only. What does remain, though, is the strong pastoral emphasis within Methodism. In each of the churches that I have responsibility for visitors still comment on the warmth of the welcome they receive and class leaders and pastoral visitors still visit faithfully. Let us be proud of this but let us also not lose sight of the other side of accountability. Let's not throw out the baby with the bath water. If we lose our concern for one another's spiritual well-being then we lose something very precious. I find it deeply ironic, therefore, that of all the churches in Raunds it is not the Methodist but the Community church, which lays greatest stress on mutual oversight and accountability. What would Mr Wesley say?

The whole period of a minister's training and probation is, of course, an exercise in being accountable and one that I have grown from. At Queens we were required to meet in small groups of our peers to reflect upon our ongoing experiences. In a group that was truly committed to one another this meant sharing the intensities of joy and pain, our fears as well as our hopes. This was in addition to the informal conversations that arose naturally over cups of coffee and games of pool as a result of sharing together in community. The process continued into the probationary years. Each of us had to journal our experiences. We were required to form a relationship with a 'mentor', an independent outsider we could confide in and who could help us reflect on what we were going through. We met regularly with other probationers and once a year with the 'dreaded' probationers' committee. I did not always enjoy it but I know that I have grown as a result.

Finally let me return to where I started. Our five year old son, like most boys of his age, is mad keen on pirates. It's not for the blood, guts, cruelty and violence. He manages to overlook this side of a pirate's demeanour. Rather it is that sense of adventure, camaraderie and working together that appeals. Dare I return to my opening illustration and say that these characterised Conference for me. It is easy to be cynical. At our last District Synod I was appointed as an elected Conference representative on a three-year term. As the ballot results were read out and my name announced I heard somebody behind me say, 'Poor chap'. Yet Conference for me was a wholly positive experience. Even if there sometimes appeared to be power-broking and unholy huddles, there was a sense of being part of a body that was representative of the Methodist people. There was a sense – as we engaged in some quite momentous business – of being guided by God into the unknown.

As we stand on the verge of a new millennium I passionately believe that Methodism does still have something distinctive to offer to the Christian Church. When I look back and wonder what John Fletcher would have made of it all I suspect that he would have encouraged us to pray for and support one another; press on after holiness and seek the Holy Spirit's guidance for the future. That will do for me.

Steve Mann

RING OF FAITH: THE CIRCUIT

A good place to start is with a definition:
'Circuit': an array of components connected so as to allow the passage of power.

'Ring': a circular band holding or connecting for identification or to sound with resonance.

'The circuit is an essential institution of Methodism.' So writes Joseph Ritson in *The Romance of Primitive Methodism*[1]. In the chapter which follows he describes the form and also the missionary function of the circuit in the nineteenth century. In the days of John Wesley the travelling preacher worked in the circuit to which he was appointed. In turn he visited the societies, enquiring after the spiritual well-being of the members and fellowship. His teaching and care was designed to encourage growth in personal spirituality and further outreach. His function was described at the first Conference in 1744: 'To feed and guide, to teach and govern the flock'[2].

In the years following the death of John Wesley in 1791 preachers were moved annually and were only allowed to remain two years in a circuit if 'remarkable revival' was taking place. Ritson also speaks of the nature and purpose of the circuit being for mutual support, security and evangelism. The strength was in a number of small societies belonging to one cohesive unit allowing successful evangelism and the development of church organisation. Essential to this development was the travelling preacher. His significance cannot be stressed enough, for he became the catalyst for growth and for the continuance of the work and mission that is the lifeblood of the Church.

But the circuit didn't just happen. In the early days a mission was planned from an established circuit into a particular neighbourhood, resulting in a gathering together of new converts and class meetings for those 'desiring to flee from the wrath to come'. Organisation and consolidation was still under the control of the parent circuit, which supplied preachers and financial help. By this time the mission would be seen as an established extension to the existing circuit. When it became strong enough in organisation and finance it became a circuit in its own right and appointed the officers which served at the Quarterly Meeting. These were a superintendent preacher, local preachers, circuit and society stewards and Sunday school superintendents. Each circuit took its name from some notable town or village within it.

John Wesley was convinced of the need for Methodist societies to be linked together if they were to grow in spiritual strength and efficacy. This was the purpose of itineracy throughout the British Isles – to consolidate and unify the Connexion as well as emphasising the fact of belonging to an ecclesiastical unity that was bigger than the local circuit.

Upon his death different styles of Methodism began to appear. There were many notable preachers who evangelised in areas as yet untouched by the Gospel. This led to new circuits emerging that possessed a different ethos and different emphases from those of John Wesley's time. The driving force of such mission and preaching was a Gospel of forgiveness and reconciliation which was encapsulated in the Great Commission:

> 'Go therefore and make disciples of all nations, baptising them in the name of the Father and of the Son and of the Holy Spirit, and teaching them to obey everything that I have commanded you.
>
> Matthew 28:19-20

The circuit in which I serve at present can bear witness to many individuals who took hold of the challenge of that Great Commission. Their contributions set up cottage meetings which in turn became classes of societies. They were men like Sammy Hick, the itinerant blacksmith of Aberford, whose portable anvil resides under the Communion table in the present chapel.

We have looked at our inheritance of faith but how does a 'Ring of Faith' demonstrate its nature at the present time? This circuit comprises twelve societies, three towns and nine villages largely situated in Wharfedale. Most of the premises are more then a hundred years old and some are close to their bicentenaries. The circuit, however, is more than property. It is the people of faith who determine the nature and the life of their circuit as they each respond to the Gospel and seek to live it out.

There are roots in every strand of Methodism from the past and they are still part of our inheritance. The design of the chapels, the place of the pulpit, the pews and the Communion area have an influence, however hidden that might be, on the way we do 'church'. Dance, drama and modern music also belong in worship, though they have not always fitted in comfortably. However, the present 'Ring of Faith' has begun to accommodate these things. We are recognising that we are richer in diversity held in tension than simply being of one tradition. There is no guarantee these days of just a 'Hymn Sandwich' in worship. This is evidence that the real treasure of being in circuit together is in valuing our differences and in assimilating them into circuit life.

The Circuit Meeting remains the hub of the organisation. Every society has a place and an opportunity to contribute. Recently we introduced a new theme to the reporting section of the agenda, entitled 'Hallelujah'. It is an invitation for any member to report on the Good News and developments within the circuit to which the meeting can then respond with a hearty 'hallelujah!' It has been known for a queue to form; there is much to report!

As the emphasis from the beginning of our meetings has been on the key role taken by our local preachers we record their positive contribution. As superintendent I rarely hear them preach but I hear about them like this . . . 'stimulating, challenging worship, well-prepared and offered with sincerity'. It prompts people to write to me or the local preachers' secretary: 'Just thought that you would like to hear about the encouraging service that Mr So-and-So led.' That does us all good. It also encourages the local preachers, making all their effort well worthwhile because someone is being blessed by God. The conversations too that result are a joy: 'I have been thinking, praying about taking a note to preach . . . Miss So-and-So got me wondering . . . perhaps God is calling me to some new service.' The 'Ring of Faith', that resonance of authenticity, is still impacting on lives. Hallelujah!

It speaks too at a Local Preachers' Recognition Service when a large circuit congregation gathers together mid-week in February. It is times like this when I hear folks say how glad they are to belong to the circuit.

In the need to further and strengthen the circuit we have arranged events many of which are reminiscent of the early days of Methodism, when the emphasis was on fellowship and spiritual growth. We held a Lovefeast, and, perhaps out of curiosity or a lack of understanding of the terminology, a big congregation gathered representative of the many societies within the circuit. It was a successful event, uplifting in the worship and praise and humbling in the testimony that was offered.

Then came the Prayer Concerts, prayer meetings that included readings, music and guidance for prayer topics. People came out of curiosity and went away encouraged. For some, participation came as a big surprise but a great joy. But the significant thing was that people felt able to talk about the particular needs of their societies and in turn promised to pray for each other. Members of chapels who had never held prayer meetings started up prayer groups as a regular event. Changes in people, in children's work, attendance and commitment to worship have been noted and attributed to the time that people began to pray together. Thus the 'Ring' that speaks of authenticity became a reality as a result of the exercised faith of the people.

The early day strategies still leave their mark within the life of many societies. When the Boston Spa Chapel was founded it received a significant financial gift from Methodists in Leeds. When recently the chapel celebrated 150 years of witness, the decision was taken to raise money to give away to encourage another chapel, a repayment which was a debt of gratitude.

One of the beneficiaries was a struggling village chapel in the circuit which had a small, mainly elderly congregation. They saw themselves as poor, devoid of energy and going it alone, and it had been suggested that they move into a neighbouring circuit. But the monetary gift, the prayers, the support for events from others in the circuit and the care of the local preachers have all improved their situation and raised their spirits. Though the congregation is still elderly, it is greater in numbers, with new members being received. They pitch in and work as a team. I enquired, 'Why the difference?' The response was, 'We feel we are loved, somebody cares about us and we belong to this circuit.' But the spin-off from this is that now in turn members give support to other circuit events.

The concept of mission also continues. Over a year ago, a local preacher on trial offered as Unit 19 of the *Faith & Worship* training course (the final piece of research undertaken on a subject of personal choice) 'A Strategy for Village Chapels'. This focused on a small society in a growing village close to major developments on the A1. The strategy was adopted by the Circuit Meeting with the promise of practical support. Five months later significant progress is apparent within different age groups and within the community.

The circuit structure also needs to be capable of adapting to meet the needs of a changing society. For example, from a larger society in the circuit outreach is being made into a new housing development. This is a place where Churches Together has very strong ties. So perhaps future development may be ecumenical and not based on a single denomination apart from the fact that our folk are involved and still need circuit support.

If this 'Ring of Faith' is to continue then its lived out expression needs to respond to the challenges of the day. This is in no way a compromise of the Gospel message but a change of vehicle to deliver it.

What does the future hold for this circuit? Preachers and ministers have always been stationed in the circuit, so, recognising that each minister brings different strengths, we are looking for ways in which these can be developed and used across the circuit for the benefit of everyone. We've offered Bible study, a series on belief and workshops on prayer.

Thus the 'Ring of Faith' sounds the genuine note that for many opens the eye of faith and leads to active Christian commitment. It was said of Adam that it was not good for him to be alone; neither is it good for a society to be isolated. Its strength is in the belonging and in being glad to identify with the whole.

A comment made recently by a circuit member sums this up: 'All I know is that when the circuit is broken the power fails to get round.'

Margaret Woodlock-Smith

Notes
1. Joseph Ritson, *The Romance of Primitive Methodism*, PM Publishing House (1909) p.205.
2. Rupert Davies, Gordon Rupp (General Editors), *A History of the Methodist Church in Great Britain (Volume One)*, Epworth Press (1965) p. 231.

RURAL, RELEVANT AND REALISTIC

The 'problems' of rural Methodism have been with us for as long as I can remember, but we have heard much less about its possibilities. We have been seduced by giantism into believing that numbers are all-important. Small may be beautiful environmentally but not, apparently, when it applies to the Christian Church. And so it is that the dominant model of the church is that of the 'programme' urban church which opens seven days a week with a 150 plus membership. This has had a most depressing effect upon rural congregations which can never hope to function like their larger suburban sisters. This is also a great tragedy. A small rural church has so much going for it and has so many strengths and virtues, and at the beginning of a new millennium we should be celebrating the small church and not burying it.

Fortunately nearly half the chapels in Methodism are designated as 'village/rural' and if you add only a small proportion of those in the 'small town' category, the figure would be over half. Furthermore, over half the chapels in Methodism have a membership of 40 or under.

There are different ways of being the church, and what is good and effective in suburbia probably will not work in the village. In towns the church building is the *locus* and the *focus* of the church's mission. In the village the *loci* and the *foci* are within the community itself. It has been suggested that whereas the appropriate symbol for the urban church is light, the appropriate symbol for the rural church is salt which dissolves into the veins and capillaries of the village community. Membership of the church is by identification rather than by participation. That is why the greatest opposition to any suggestion that the chapel should be closed will come from people who never, or rarely, attend. They may come to the Harvest Festival, at Christmas or Easter and they will be there in force for the funerals (often the largest congregation of the year). They will feel a strong affinity with the chapel which holds many memories but weekly attendance does not appeal. They are like the fickle football supporter who will go to the cup matches but is not interested in the weekly league matches. Even so the average church attendance in a village will represent a much higher percentage of the population than will be found in the most 'successful' urban church. Research has shown that a staggeringly high proportion of the village (sometimes up to 80 per cent) will have been inside church or chapel at some time during the year. No urban church could claim those figures. The congregation of 12 in Little Piddlington is an effective unit compared to many larger urban churches.

A small rural church is not a failed large church, just as a tangerine is not a failed orange. The small village chapel has its own style, its own integrity. It is plain, intimate and personal. It is where the most important decisions are made between church council meetings!

For the rural church the changes over the last 50 years have been profound. Most of the potential leadership of those who were young in the middle of the century was exported to towns and cities as occupational opportunities grew less in the countryside. The new leadership in fact has been supplied by the retired and the early-retired immigrants. Elderly congregations have been replaced by slightly less elderly ones and the mournful predictions of 40 years ago that our elderly rural congregations would die out within 10 to 15 years have been proved wrong.

The social and economic impact made upon the village communities by the arrival of more affluent people is receiving a great deal of attention. Some have argued that most rural ills can be laid at the door of the incomer. After all (it is claimed) they have inflated the cost of housing so that local people can no longer afford to live in the village. Because they have their own car(s) and a deep freeze they do not bother with the local shop but go to the supermarket. And because of their age they are no longer producing children for the village school so that closes too. They have their own transport so they do not use the public bus service which deteriorates to the point of virtual extinction. What they do want is street lighting, leylandii hedges and for farmers to keep their cattle and muddy tractors off their grass verges. They are criticised by local people for not getting involved in community events, but when they do they are accused of trying to take over the place. They are also totally opposed to any more development in the village, either of housing or industrial units. It is, of course, impolitic to point out that it was the local people who sold the houses in the first place, and that local people have been using supermarkets for years anyway, and that 2.4 children applies to the countryside as well as to the towns, and so a few families can no longer maintain a whole school – or chapel!

As we enter a new millennium the rural church can face the future with some confidence and hope but only, I believe, if certain principles are followed.

The first is that the newcomers must be welcomed. Where rural churches are growing today it is because they have responded to the needs of the newcomers. In Methodist terms it is quite clear what has happened. The new people have been warmly welcomed into the life of the church and have also been invited to take up positions of leadership and responsibility. The six year rule has not penetrated to every corner of Methodism in rural areas and if you have been senior steward and treasurer for 50 years it isn't easy to give that up. Similarly if you have been sitting, perhaps in an increasingly arthritic condition, on the organ stool for 50 years it is still not easy to give up the place to a younger newcomer. Such actions need grace but where grace has triumphed exciting things have begun to happen.

Another characteristic of the developing rural chapel is that it has transformed its Victorian image. One of the familiar tales of the countryside is that of the young Methodist family who move to a village and attend the chapel eagerly on the first Sunday. There they experience cultural shock. Nothing much has changed for 100 years and there is no ministry for the children. The next Sunday they are off in their car to the Methodist church in the nearest market town centre where they will feel very much at home. The progressive rural chapel, however, has transformed its interior which is now warm and comfortable and welcoming. Probably the central pulpit has gone and space created, and the pews have been replaced by comfortable chairs (especially if the former were of the austere and penitential kind). Usually a modern kitchen and toilets have been added. The noticeboard is up-to-date and the grounds are well kept. The congregation also takes far more interest in the quality of its worship. It does not necessarily mean that guitars have replaced the organ or that *Mission Praise* reigns supreme. Neither does it necessarily mean a charismatic take-over, it means simply that people are taking worship seriously and that both the style and the substance have been improved.

One of the attractions of village life for urban people is that they feel they are coming into a human-sized community which has roots. Thus the parish church in its present state is acceptable to many new people simply because it is old and probably rather beautiful. The fact that it is cold, draughty and uncomfortable hardly seems to register. The 19th century Victorian chapel, on the other hand, is not old enough to be respectable, it is only old enough to be anachronistic. Thus, whilst the parish church can rejoice in its antiquity, the Methodist chapel has to concentrate on modernity to fit it for the new millennium.

The second principle must be ecumenical. In the past this has been resisted by many small Methodist congregations because they believe it would result in the closure of the chapel. This need not necessarily be the case, although it is right to question whether or not it might be within the purposes of God for the chapel to close. In fact, compared with the parish church, the Methodist chapel is often far more suitable for the mission of the Church. It is smaller, cheaper to maintain and heat, and has a more flexible usefulness. In Loddon in Norfolk, the parish church is used during the summer and the Methodist church is used during the winter.

But ecumenism is about far more than the rationalisation of buildings. It is about a vision of the people of God as one family sharing the whole of their Christian life together including worship, which is the most difficult of all ecumenical nuts to crack. This means acknowledging that diversity is just as important as unity and that they are really inseparable. Like the village shop, therefore, if the ecumenical village church/chapel is to survive it must sell everything – and be open at hours that people find convenient. This is not to suggest that every service should be a liturgical pot-pourri. It is to suggest, however, that a mixed diet of worship is possible over a period of one month (say) and that, in love, people will learn in time to join in services which at first seem strange and foreign to them.

The third principle must be that of the re-emergence of strong local lay leadership. Methodism has always proudly claimed this to be its heritage but in fact we are as priest-ridden as any church in Christendom. The need to rediscover and re-activate a strong, vibrant lay leadership culture is being discussed in all denominations. But that's as far as it's got! There is a pressing need to act. 'God moves in a mysterious way' and it may well be that the difficulties in maintaining the present structures may make changes inevitable. The Church of England is no longer able to plan for a parson in every village (not that it has ever succeeded). There will have to be (sooner rather than later) a recognition and implementation of lay leadership at local level even though it causes tensions and can provide a real threat to ordained people. Methodists, of course, should have no such fear – even though we have! The Conference Report on the Ministry of the People of God in the World is still worth reading.

The fourth principle is to work for a renewed community rather than for a full church. This is the recognition that the mission of the Christian Church is not about filling pews but about transforming the world. The rural church will continue to have a marvellous opportunity to influence the quality of life in the communities in which it is set. The contemporary rural community faces hidden poverty and deprivation, a lack of access to essential services, unemployment and a chronic housing shortage for people on low incomes. The village church is ideally placed to act as catalyst, initiator, and/or co-ordinator to enable community action to develop locally. This is already happening in many rural situations. Where there is a community transport scheme, an emergency help service, a shopping rota, a relief system for carers, drop-in centres, children's groups and so on – there you will usually find strong church participation and leadership.

The fifth principle is that as a Church we enter fully into the ethical debates which are now centred upon food production, the environment and bio-technology. The evidence is mounting that there is no one simple or simplistic answer to the many ethical dilemmas thrown up in these areas. The essential thing is for the Christian Church to respond theologically. But theology isn't only (or mainly) derived from books. It is rooted in experience. The rural church is in the front line with its links with and pastoral care for the farming community. Much of the environmental debate is focused upon farming methods and development plans for the countryside. Bio-technology, the cloning of animals and Genetically Modified Organisms, in addition to animal welfare concerns and the access issue all underline the key part the rural church has to play in the coming of the new millennium.

The final principle must be about the nature of community itself but is in the form of a question. Is there something fundamentally Christian about human-sized communities? Is community possible in megalopolis? How important is it to live in a place where you are known and to which you belong, and to be a member of a church in which you can be missed?

John Clarke

THE SUBURBAN CHURCH

The Word became flesh and lived among us . . .
> John 1:14

But each of us was given grace according to the measure of Christ's gift . . . The gifts he gave were that some would be apostles, some prophets, some evangelists, some pastors and teachers, to equip the saints for the work of ministry, for building up the body of Christ, until all of us come to the unity of the faith and of the knowledge of the Son of God, to maturity, to the measure of the full stature of Christ.
> Ephesians 4:7 and 11-13

All churches seek to embody God's love in the place where they are, and core elements of ministry – worship, service, fellowship and outreach – are common to them all. But the way in which such ministry is lived out will vary simply because the setting of each church and congregation is different. I would like to share some of the experiences of ministry I have had in recent years, looking firstly at ministry based around the local church building, and secondly at the church's ministry to the local community.

For many years the church building has been seen as 'a sign of the Gospel'. Where communities have grown significantly churches have often been adapted or expanded; extra space has been created so that worship can be more flexible, and so that the building can be used to greater effect. A lay worker once said of his church: 'This church was packed in the 1950s for two hours of worship a week; we are now exercising Christian ministry seven days a week.' It has been my privilege to serve in churches which have been extended, modernised and redeveloped 'to serve the present age'.

Worship can be very varied! The congregation of a large church may include people of different ages, personalities and spiritualities. As a result Methodist worship is very diverse, often incorporating a variety of musical resources, drama, mime and dance. This is also true of the central act of worship, the Holy Communion. Some congregations still share the bread and wine 'table by table', to reflect the gathering of the first disciples and fellowship together; others feel it more appropriate to have continuous Communion as an expression of our 'oneness'. The new *Methodist Worship Book* will give the Church a wide range of rich worship resources.

Worship in our churches is further enriched by the ministry of local preachers, who bring their experience of life and faith into their preaching and leading of worship. In some churches members of the congregation are also worship leaders. They prepare services with the preacher and can bring their own gifts and their knowledge of the congregation into leading some of the worship. Some churches now offer two different kinds of service on Sunday mornings, and some also hold mid-week services for people who find it difficult to attend on Sunday, or who prefer a quieter, more reflective act of worship. Worship matters to people, and sometimes tensions can result because people have varied backgrounds and temperaments. As we look to the future, our churches will be greatly blessed if we can bring together all that God's Spirit gives us, growing together 'so that the body of Christ may be built up'.

In addition to worship on Sunday, the suburban church in many places is busy all through the week. Smaller groups meet together, often in homes, and the titles – Bible Study, Midweek Fellowship, Open To Question, Prayer Meeting – reflect the way in which Christians today explore their discipleship Some groups within churches also find encouragement from attending local or national events such as Spring Harvest and Easter People, or lecture series and ecumenical events. Groups also meet to share interests such as music and drama, arts and crafts, all of which help to bring people together within their churches. Work amongst young people is also a priority for many congregations, and they provide a range of activities for various age groups. Whatever may be our personal view, Sunday is often not the best day for work among young people, and mid-week meetings, or after-school clubs, may be effective in reaching children who would not normally attend Sunday worship.

The circuit system within Methodism fosters a unique sense of fellowship between church congregations, who can learn from one another. The rural church can remind others that the harvest is not always 'safely gathered in' without a great deal of hard work and worry, while the larger, suburban church can share its skills and resources – for example, finance, property and music – with smaller congregations.

We now turn to the ministry of the church in the wider community, both in joining with people from other churches in ecumenical witness and, as importantly, in reaching out to people who have no connection with any church.

Some services of worship, perhaps those which involve schoolchildren, can take place away from church buildings, in a school or community centre. This enables larger numbers of people to attend, and those people who are not used to going to church, or who may feel uneasy about doing so, may feel encouraged to attend in a more relaxed, neutral setting. Many churches join together for united acts of witness, for instance at Christmas and Easter, or they may join forces and finance to provide services for different groups, such as a lunch club for the elderly. This kind of activity is very much in the Wesley tradition of going to meet people to serve them where they are.

The local church should also seek new ways in which its buildings can be used to help groups in the local community, as new needs arise and as existing ones develop. If it is in touch with the community the church will be aware of problems as they occur and be able to offer help. For example, a church in Newcastle has been involved in two innovative projects, one to support the carers of sufferers from Alzheimer's disease, and another to enable unemployed people to learn clerical and office skills to help them in their search for work.

Churches are often in a position to give financial resources to a variety of causes at home and overseas. Indeed some set aside a proportion of their annual income for this purpose and this can amount to thousands of pounds.

Many stories could be told of how the members of local churches seek to bear witness and live out the Gospel in the places where they live and work. In one large village most of the members of the parish council were also members of local churches. Once when a school governors' meeting ended early, a third of those present went straight on to an ecumenical Lent course. In a town where concern over vandalism led to a packed public meeting, a Youth and Community Association was established to respond creatively to the needs of young people. The local churches all became involved and gave much needed financial backing to the group in its early days; the Anglican Church donated all the proceeds from its flower festival. In congregations I have served members have been involved in at least 35 voluntary organisations, charities, campaign groups and political parties, not infrequently in leadership positions. Involvement in such organisations is a vital part of ministry in the world.

There is a great deal of caring and visiting in communities which is undertaken by local church members. Flowers can be sent to people at special times (such as birthdays, anniversaries, moving into a new home) or at difficult times (such as illness or bereavement). The church can be a healing community where those who have had a difficult time can find God's love through friendship and fellowship. Housebound members of a church community still exercise a wonderful ministry through prayer, telephone calls, writing letters and simply being themselves. A lady in a nursing home told me of how the staff often pop in to see her for a chat and to share their problems, and I know it is because they are sure they will be treated with Christian kindness and their confidences respected. Pastoral care is given as well as received.

In the context of pastoral support the rites of passage must not be overlooked. Sensitive help, care and guidance can be given at baptisms, weddings and funerals, but the church ceremony is only part of the church's care. The cradle roll and the offer of parenting classes, marriage preparation and continuing friendship after the wedding, bereavement support and visiting, are all ways in which churches can seek to support homes and families at significant times.

Church members can also witness and exercise their discipleship in the workplace. For those who have paid employment, a large part of their time is spent at work, and there are opportunities to give a Christian standpoint on issues of honesty, integrity, justice and industrial relations. A firm stand on such issues is not easily forgotten. I recall a rather bleary-eyed conversation in a canning factory at 3am, when an engineer told me of 'Old Fred, 'e were a Methodist lay preacher; 'e never pinched anything, not even a strawberry, and treated everyone the same.' Here was a man whose Christian discipleship on the shop floor still impressed his colleagues years after he had left.

In some churches members are in positions of considerable influence in their working lives, often bearing great responsibilities. I have been the minister of head teachers, bankers, a hospital consultant, the managing director of a very large local company and the general secretary of a trade union – all of whose decisions can affect the lives of hundreds, perhaps thousands, of people. The church needs to give support and encouragement, and perhaps the opportunity to discuss their daily work, so that their discipleship can be more effective. A senior deacon once said to me, 'I think the Church should ask nothing of those in positions of demanding responsibility, but just give them the help they need.'

It is true that people experience difficulty in trying to serve the local church as well as exercising their discipleship in the wider world, and this is also true for ministers. An ecumenical Lent course in Scotland once contained these words: 'It is not the task of the laity to help the minister to run the church: it is the task of the minister to help the laity to change the world!' In the future more attention could be given to equipping the laity to 'change the world', whether in the church, the home, the community or the place of work.

The Church is not perfect; the old adage says, 'If you find the perfect church, don't join it, because you will spoil it!' Yet in many places the local church seeks to dwell among its community as a sign of the Gospel, and to reach out to express God's love to all people within that community. My prayer is that the body may be built up, and that God's people may be equipped for work in his service.

Andrew Foster

IN THE CITY, OUT OF LOVE

I did not choose the title of this chapter, but I respond to it warmly. My first experience of inner-city life was in Notting Hill, London. It was there that I first fell in love with the inner city. Physically the area was poor, run-down and delapidated, as many fine old houses were falling into decay, with plaster and paint peeling away. A large number of the most decrepit houses were owned by Rachman clones, who divided them up into poor standard accommodation and filled them with newly-arrived West Indians who lived in damp, cold, cramped, expensive and overcrowded conditions.

But church life was wonderful, for me and for many of the West Indians who joined the church. At Notting Hill, in the days of the trinity of the Revs Denny, Ainger and Mason, there was a church life which was intellectually stimulating and emotionally warm for all ethnic groups. It offered a spirituality available to all, and a sense of community which united people into lifelong friendships and involvement with the life of the church. It was a church in which many ethnic groups found the first accepting welcome they had experienced in England.

How different Notting Hill looks today! Peeling stucco, Rachmanism, and cramped living conditions have substantially disappeared. The part-time brothel across the road from where I lived is once again an elegant and very expensive town house, I am sure no longer of ill repute. Money has poured into the area, council houses have been sold off or renovated, and many 1960s black residents have moved further out of London, or returned home to the Caribbean. Notting Hill has become a most desirable place for the wealthy to live.

The church is still a lively and innovative community, having benefited from creative leadership, lay and ministerial. Its smaller congregation still has a strong Caribbean membership but it is a 'mature' membership rather than a new one.

Methodist churches in other parts of London are now experiencing what may be the beginning of a similar pattern of church expansion, as West Africans move into new areas of the inner city. Walworth, for example, which had virtually no members 25 years ago, now has the largest membership in the London South-East District. Membership at Bermondsey, a mile away, has grown from 46 to 180 in 12 years.

The new black members are mainly well-educated, have high aspirations for themselves and their families, and welcome leadership roles, if they are really allowed to lead! Two views can be taken on this. The more cynical one is that this time the remaining whites are numerically much weaker than 30 years ago, so they have in the main surrendered leadership because they could do no other. A more hopeful view is that both ministers and members have learned something from the widespread failures of the white-led churches to welcome and work with Caribbean Methodists 30 years ago, and now actively encourage black leadership. However, even now white racism can still rear its hideous head in the churches, and it is all the more evil because it ignores all we should have learned in the last 30 years.

Whatever the future holds, it is high time that the Methodist Church as a whole recognised the crucial and valuable contribution to church life played by those of Caribbean and African origin in inner-city churches. If we are serious in what we say about the missionary role of the lay people of the Church, we must acknowledge that inner-city Methodism and city life as a whole is benefiting from the biggest influx of 'missionaries from overseas' that this country has ever seen. I put the words 'missionaries from overseas' in inverted commas because it is an expression we do not use now, but I expressed it this way to make a point. In many inner-city situations there would not be a worshipping Methodist church if it were not for these revitalised congregations. They not only fill our churches, they bring a warmth, passion and 'raw energy' to the worshipping life of the church. They also live out committed Christian lives in the various work situations in which they find themselves. Their contribution deserves to be publicised and honoured.

Meanwhile, several inner-city areas are beginning to go through a physical cycle of change similar to that in Notting Hill. The engine of change this time has been the 1980s sale of council housing and new private developments. In Bermondsey the Council is 'considering' plans to sell off three large 1950s blocks of council housing to a private developer, who wants to build more luxury apartments for city workers. There is always a danger that urban renewal, (I do not use the nasty word 'gentrification') comes at the cost of continuing pressure on affordable social housing. In 20 or 30 years' time, if this process has continued, what will be its effect on the mainly black members who presently live in council housing? Will the current growth come to an end as it has in Notting Hill? Certainly evidence suggests that the churches are no more successful at holding the second generation of young Africans (now black British) than they were with second generation Caribbean young people.

It is almost as easy to glamorise inner-city life as it is to demonise it. Because so much is written about city life in the second category (drugs, crime, violence, graffiti, racial tension, unemployment) all of which cannot be denied, I want to emphasise something about the positive side of inner-city life. A few years ago I took a group of local preachers on a tour of an inner-city area. My instructions were that they were responsible for preaching the sermon the next morning on 'Signs of the Kingdom'. As they walked around they were asked to look out for signs of the kingdom, in streets which felt hostile and alien to many of them, and to report on what they saw. The sermon the next morning was full of signs: young black and white youngsters playing happily together; a bit of graffiti, 'Jesus Christ is Lord'; a young person helping an elderly person across the road; corner shops which are still centres of community; tiny, but carefully tended, gardens full of plants; a notice about the opening of a new pensioners' lunch club; bustling streets that felt safe to walk along because there were so many people about, and so on.

A recent poster outside our church said, 'This is not a God forsaken world.' Christians in the inner city must view what everyone else sees with different eyes, or in Charles Handy's phrase, they must 'frame the familiar picture in a new way' so they see the picture differently. When you see the picture differently you respond to what you see in a different way. If you believe that God exhibits as much concern for the city as he does for the countryside, you will look for signs of his activity as eagerly as you might look for signs of spring on a February country walk.

Signs of the activity of God and God's people have traditionally been associated with the mission work of inner-city Missions. The South London Mission, for example, was established as the result of the Forward Movement over 100 years ago in an area of breathtaking poverty, overcrowding, immorality and criminality. Its 'hands-on' social work, from serving soup to hundreds out of dustbins (presumably new ones), to breakfasts for school children, and the care of the elderly, are part of the legend of the area. But what is the future of social work today? If the churches are fuller on a Sunday than they have been for many years, the Monday-to-Saturday social work is generally declining. The old 'go it alone' patterns of social work helping the 'poor and needy' are dying out.

Missions are now often drained of the resources of volunteers and money. They can no longer decide what they will do without reference to others working in the area. Attempts at partnerships and alliances have had a very chequered history as local authority cut-backs, or the sudden withdrawals of support from charities, have led to the collapse of projects, with resulting painful redundancies and sometimes a deep sense of betrayal. The wearying rounds of monitoring, chasing up three-year limited grants, and trying to reshape what you want to do in order to fit the latest criteria of a charitable body or local authority, have all sapped the energy, enthusiasm and creativity of many inner-city Missions.

As inner-city areas are changing perhaps it is necessary that the old concept of the 'Mission' must be killed before it becomes a killer itself. At the South London Mission we are trying to ask the question, what would it mean to change from 'Mission' to 'mission'? How can our activities truly reflect the needs and the priorities of the community, and come from the community? Meanwhile the gap between the black Sunday congregation and the mainly elderly white, non-church attending, recipients of traditional Mission support Monday-to-Friday, is only very slowly being addressed. Slowly, more black members are being involved in Mission activities, and Mission activities are beginning to reflect the needs of a new black community. A Work and School Partnership (with the rather unfortunate acronym in a black context of WASP) helped many black school leavers over a number of years, but had to close down when Local Authority money was withdrawn. More recently a Saturday Supplementary School has been started with nearly 30 children aged from five to eight receiving extra teaching and help with the 'three Rs'. The school has only been able to start because of financial support from churches and individuals all over the country, which is more reliable than other sources of income. Such projects may be pointers to the future.

I am aware that this is a very personal and individualistic contribution, but as I was given the title I can hardly write a piece which is remote and objective. Therefore I want to end with a very brief expression of the theology which guides (or is it drives?) me. Perceptive readers will have picked up clues to it in every line of this brief article. It is an incarnational theology. God revealed his unique presence among us in Jesus, who was born homeless in a city. The Word was made flesh and dwelt among us. The Good News of God's presence is preached when a young child is liberated to learn to read and write; when a homeless person receives a gift of food; when a newcomer to this country is offered warm, secure, affordable housing; and when humanity is shown in a welcome, a smile and an offer of friendship. An incarnational theology needs to be preached in word and deed in city and countryside, in suburb and town, but I am grateful to be able to try to work it out, 'In the City, out of Love'.

John Lampard

NO MID-LIFE CRISIS HERE!
A VIEW FROM THE MIDDLE YEARS

Conscious of my own passage of time, I noticed the board game 'Mid-Life Crisis' on the stall at a church jumble sale. There were hoots of laughter and pithy comments as I paid up and made my purchase. I purposefully tucked my new acquisition under my arm, determined that it must not be lost. Arriving home, I suggested to my family that we should play the game to discover if I fitted into the pressures of reaching 50! Indeed, the game was played twice. The suggestions of cracking up, divorce and bankruptcy all seemed inappropriate for me. I didn't fit into these particular circumstances and situations. There was more chance of raising my blood pressure from the thought of playing it a third time! The game is now ready to be returned to the next jumble sale for another 50 year old to check out their crisis!

I don't consider that I am at a crisis point in my life, though my hair has a particular seasonal look – speckled with frost! Hopefully, the signs of distinction will overwhelm the signs of extinction! Thornton's toffee can now only be sucked and never chewed! My spectacles are changed more frequently, and I have to remember to say 'Pardon?' rather than the glib 'What did you say?' I remember that I considered youth to be eternal, but now an active connection with Methodist Homes seems very relevant!

I have always been struck by the Gospel writers' revelation of the amazing focus and energy Jesus displayed during his earthly ministry. This same experience is recognised in those who followed him and were commissioned to go into all the world to share the Good News of his kingdom. The power to fulfil Christ's will and way for them was confirmed through the gift of the Holy Spirit at Pentecost. Followers of Christ through the centuries have often revealed the same force and focus. Surely John Wesley was of this tradition? There were signs in him of one who was driven by God in the work of ministry. He stood up to those who ridiculed him, and to physical dangers. He stood firm and was strong in his faith. It could be argued that his drive of faith caused limitations in other aspects of his life, but it brought a great deal of good into the lives of those who responded to his preaching and into the life of our nation.

A Methodist upbringing could so easily have meant for me an easy acceptance of faith and denomination without the struggle of personal questions and doubts. It was the recognition of a spirituality with social justice within the Methodist tradition that fired my faith. I realise that you can't be a passive believer; you belong to a living God, who has a purpose for you. Your relationship with God includes you in the same purpose and pattern of life as Christ's, when he lived on earth. You are a contributor for good. The Good News which asks you to participate and asks you to be a link in the chain of believers is an exciting though demanding experience. There is something so awe-inspiring and thrilling about the God who loves you so much that his only Son came to die for you. This love of God inspires you to love and serve others.

You actually want to live it out and give it out. The other day, as I was leaving a church in my circuit, I looked up and saw the words above the door which were from James 1:22: 'Be doers of the word, and not hearers only, deceiving yourselves.' It was a parting challenge for the worshippers. I just hoped they always looked up before they went out!

In the Wesleyan tradition there is a great emphasis and enthusiasm for action and involvement with other people. You are not allowed to pass by on the other side, to stand on the sidelines, to turn a blind eye or a deaf ear. You have to engage in bringing about the change for good. This is clearly set out in John Wesley's Rule for Christian Living:

> Do all the good you can,
> By all the means you can,
> In all the ways you can,
> In all the places you can,
> At all the times you can,
> To all people you can,
> As long as ever you can.

We use sayings to sustain ourselves and inspire others such as, 'Maximise your opportunities for the glory of God.' However, there is a cost involved as well as a commitment. Indeed, many children will tell of parents who spend more time helping others than being with their own families. Some spouses and children have been put off the Christian Faith because of the tired members of their family who return home to them totally worn out, unable to hear the voices and needs of their own household.

Some years ago, I was introduced to the concept of the 'reflective practitioner'. It confirmed the teaching I received in theological college of reviewing your ministry and life on a regular basis. You, as a person, are valued, and you must have a realistic understanding of your commitment and purpose in life. If you pour yourself out in service and pastoral care of others, so you in turn must be personally nourished and renewed. I was conscious that as a single person the term 'married to the church' fitted me well and was used to describe me by my family and friends. Such expectations, either perceived or expected, can actually reduce your ability to serve God effectively. Therefore the demands on you, and the level of service you are able to offer, have to be examined in a reflective and prayerful way. Relationships may have to be re-evaluated, and, where hurt and damage exists, repair and renewal must take place. Family and friends matter, for how we relate to them is a sign to others of our faith and service. Space for the development of the individual must always be acknowledged, for didn't Christ take time to 'go apart and rest a while'?

In our personal pilgrimage and service we often focus upon ourselves, reflecting upon what we can contribute and the commitment that we can make. But growth and maturity in faith enable us to realise the importance of belonging to a community or body of believers. Together we share and contribute our gifts, skills and ministries, and working as a team is enriching and enabling. The ability to accept strengths and weaknesses in a relationship of trust and respect is both exciting and liberating. We are no longer alone and in isolation, but part of the worshipping and serving people of God.

The privilege of partnership also brings the experience of great pain through loss and parting caused by death. We live in the hope and trust of life eternal through Christ, and we discover the intimacy of the resurrection in so many partings. The departure of family, friends, members of your congregation and community add to those of trusted and respected colleagues and role models. The influence of their life and death on you is significant and often more than they could have imagined.

With the passing of the years you are also aware of disappointment within yourself. The times of not matching the expectation, the inadequacy of preparation and the failed presentation. You know what it is to walk down the pulpit steps asking for forgiveness for your halting and faltering preaching. You know the times of being the barrier and not the bridge. You are aware of the promised visits and pastoral sensitivities sadly missed. Yet from your failure and wounded spirit forgiveness gives you a renewed hope. As you lean on Christ you actively learn to draw from him new strength and changed ways. You again become the clay in the potter's hands being remodelled and remade.

No mid-life crisis here! Instead, there is a day-to-day evaluation of personal purpose in Christ's way. Pushing ourselves to breaking point proves nothing except our mortality! The dynamic of the divine is God's desire for us to love him and to serve him. We should be excited by new opportunities of service in partnership with others. In mid-life one also knows that, 'He can with me – he can without me!'

Mary Bailey

NO BANANA REPUBLIC
A DISTRICT VIEW

Some time ago it was stated that Methodist districts are figments of the connexional imagination, or perhaps nowadays an idea born out of virtual reality. They are certainly something, and the something is that which exists as a strata of Methodism between Methodist Church House and connexional desks and teams, and the grass roots of local circuit life. It may be the jam in the middle which stimulates the appetite and makes the whole more appealing and digestible, or a thin layer spread around for purely decorative purposes.

What is certainly true is that districts exist, though the present shapes and the posts of separated chairmen and chairwomen are products of our own lifetime. Indeed, the title of chairman was originally 'District Evangelist and Chairman'.

The district I know best encompasses three counties and parts of seven others. It exists in five of the nine new Regional Development Authorities, but modestly we have to say we have no presence in either Wales or Scotland.

Irrespective of which district we think of, they hold many things in common, and I now simply describe the one I know best. The first essential feature of a district is that it is a place where vision is larger than the local church and yet the vision and the dream are still accessible. The vision includes the telling of stories, especially at larger gatherings like Synod, which can be inspirational or full of educational power. It is a place where boundaries that have been drawn by circuits can be removed and we can leap-frog inspirationally from one place to another. It is a place of togetherness when in large numbers, and united worship, we are aware that the Church is still strong and that people from all walks of life share a common identity. It is a place where business can be discussed, information can be shared, new hope can be engendered and spirits can be revived. So I really do thank God for the sense of vision that a district can incarnate.

Then, of course, there is that whole cluster of ideas that can be described as Training and Fellowship. Within the district the superintendents will meet together *en bloc*, or in small county clusters. They, who excerise a pastoral oversight of the local ministers themselves, will meet in the presence of their own pastor. At the other end of experience the probationers will also meet in district groups. Rarely will a circuit have more than one probationer, but coming together with their peers and sharing in learning and training together is part of the growth process of ministry. The district handles similar events for lay workers and other specialist groups like Network and Youth and Education. Those seeking to explore their call to ministry would also meet within the district and most districts will provide residential times for ministerial renewal, refreshment and reflection. All these and more are easily encompassed in that middle layer somewhere between the top and the bottom.

One of the more exciting areas of district work is funding mission and resourcing people. We have been able to establish modest funds where people come before property, and mission is given precedence over maintenance. At the moment we are helping to fund five quite distinct appointments where people are working on the boundaries of the Church connecting with society, reaching into youth culture, and planting new congregations. This is partly because connexional generosity is matched by district commitment, but also because people are used as resources as their expertise and knowledge is made available beyond a local circuit boundary.

The district is also the focus of a realistic ecumenical presence. Methodism needs to be committed to, and fully involved in, all ecumenical conversations and this is best achieved by having a representative figure who in some ways can speak for Methodism, as a bishop speaks for Anglicanism, or a moderator for the United Reformed Church. It would be difficult to think that where one representative from the other denominations were to meet in an ecumenical gathering that they would expect to be faced by the daunting prospect of a dozen Methodist superintendents!

Pastoral care is part of the district ethos. Ministers and deacons and lay workers give themselves, often prodigally, to the needs of others by caring, walking alongside, supporting, sustaining. But they themselves are in need of renewal and refreshment. Within the district the chairman or chairwoman is normally the focal point of visiting the manses, as well as caring on behalf of the Connexion for those who have retired and those who have been bereaved within the ministerial family.

However, the most incredible thing about the district for me is that when the 33 representatives of our 33 districts sit down together for a meeting to organise the annual stationing, within one room, at that one moment, the people present have a personal knowledge of every Methodist minister in the Connexion, of every Methodist circuit in the country and, sometimes, of virtually every one of the 6,000 Methodist chapels scattered between the Isles of Scilly and the Shetland Isles. It is factual reality that by their constant travel, their pastoral oversight, and their commitment to preaching and worship, they have an incredibly wide, though not infallible, grasp of the whole picture. It means that the districts are exercising a personal care and supervision, and therefore the overall planning and missionary strategy of the Church can move forward with a sense of personal knowledge, commitment and care, rather than the blind choices of the sophisticated but impersonal computer.

I don't believe for a moment that the district is an easy concept, or that it has a great appeal to many people. Left to themselves many members of the Church would move towards a congregational model of church where one building and one congregation provide their horizons of faith. I dare believe, however, that the district offers a more missionary and visionary concept of church, a wider sense of the kingdom, a more stimulating environment for growth, a more scriptural basis for the sharing of our resources. 'From each according to their means, to each according to their needs.'

Eddie Lacy

WEARING WELL!

I've been very blessed. For 40 years I've served as a Methodist minister. My eight appointments have all been very different but each one has had its own joys and blessings. I am grateful to John Wesley and to those first Methodists; grateful to ministers and Sunday school teachers and friends who led me to Jesus, to hear God's call and to enter the ministry; grateful to Bill Sangster, Leslie Weatherhead, Donald Soper, Norman Snaith and Raymond George at the beginning and to Donald English and so many others at the end. In gratitude I sense I have a charge to keep! In this short essay, I want to share that charge with you as we look forward to another thousand years of faith.

Keep the Connexion! My spell checker won't accept that spelling – perhaps that reflects the particularity of it all. When I was at Linacre Mission nearly forty years ago a young woman named Jessie returned from college. She found that the Mission was no longer 'home' to her, and the family home had grown smaller as two young brothers had grown bigger. 'Mr Hayman,' she said, 'I've been appointed to a librarian's job in Preston. Could you help me with accommodation?' I went home and consulted the Minutes of Conference. The minister who had served at Headingley Church during my college days was now in Preston. I rang him. In no time at all, she was accommodated – with the Sunday school superintendent. She fell in love with the son, and they married and have lived happily ever since. As I took my place at the Conference Service at Newcastle in 1993, a voice said, 'Are you *the* Michael Hayman?' It was my young Liverpudlian – thirty years on. We hugged each other in welcome. I heard all about her life and family and how she was now Network Secretary for her district! The next year at the Derby Conference her husband found me, shook my hand warmly and thanked me. It's a small story, but it shows that we are all part of each other. The body needs hands and feet. The continuity of the Connexion depends on each one of us.

You may have noticed that ministers don't move as often as they used to do, and because of removal costs they don't move as far. Forty years of ministry is an exceptional hope these days as the average age for entering training for ministry is about forty years old. Keeping the Connexion alive is down to you and me! Take an interest in the wider Church.

I charge you to keep on seeking unity. This Methodist never tires of the text John Wesley quoted in his sermon on 'The Catholic Spirit', 'If your heart is right with my heart, give me your hand!' I have found it unfortunate that a Decade of Evangelism has moved Churches further apart. We have been 'spoiling' with one another over doctrine, church order and evangelistic techniques. The success of the Alpha course across many denominations hides the articulate and honest questions of the individual believer. The tension between the catholic and evangelical wings of the churches, seen in our use of scripture, women priests and flying bishops, the redefining of the Mass/Eucharist/Holy Communion; all seem designed to shut out and separate rather than bring us together. In September 1998 the General Secretary of The World Council of Churches, Rev Dr Konrad Raiser, confessed that after 50 years they had failed in their mission of unity. How clearly I recall Dr Leslie Weatherhead, as President in 1955, telling our Church that we were a bridge between the denominations.

Of course, times have changed. Now we live in a multi-racial society, with peoples from many nations with many faiths and none. The institutional racism, that inhabits so many lives, so that our own hearts and minds fail to see it and fail to see and feel the hurt, only makes the divisions deeper and more obvious.

I have a wish, a prayer, a plan for the first decade of the new millennium. Let us have a decade of loving. I'm not talking about 'flower power', I'm saying, 'Let's stop warring, arguing, battling, evangelising, and let's start loving. Start living and loving in the agape, creative and proactive, loving way of our Parent God.' It is a simple truth, spelt out in an important booklet on discipleship, but it matters: 'More people are in church because of friendship than for any other reason.' Let's get loving! Give me your hand – and reach out to hold other hands, for Christ's sake!

I was going to say, 'Keep our structures', but anyone involved in church committees and their ramifications would not forgive me.

I think we all appreciated the freeing of our structures encouraged by Rev Ronald Hoar when he was President in 1991-2, but there are dangers. If our structures and officers are not similar then there is a real danger that we can no longer talk together or support one another. The new connexional structures are making districts feel unnecessary, and the direct link with churches breaks down the picture of the circuit as the unit of Methodism. So let me say, 'Keep the circuit.' Other denominations are finding the necessity for and value of such groupings. 'From each according to his abilities, to each according to his need,' is attributed to Karl Marx, but John Wesley already knew its value. We are here for one another: we bring our gifts that all may share. The first casualties if we lose our circuits will be the smaller village churches so crucial to our life – and most Methodist churches have a membership less than 30! At all costs we must not lose sight of the fact that we need one another – we are 'connected' here as well.

Keep our Methodist understanding of 'ministry' and the priesthood of all believers. The Deed of Union says, in Methodism's own Clause 4, 'No priesthood exists which belongs exclusively to a particular order or class . . . for the sake of church order, and not because of any priestly virtue inherent in the office, the ministers are set apart by ordination to the ministry of the word and sacraments.' I was intrigued when the Report on the Church brought to Conference in 1995, 'Called to Love and Praise', redefined the term as 'the priesthood of all the believers', presumably with the emphasis on 'when we are all together'.

At Easter People one year there was a large response to an appeal for people to come forward and give themselves to Christ. A young woman stepped out of her place just in front of us and stood weeping in the queue. Her tears touched our hearts and I recall how our daughter, Stephanie, nearest to the aisle, went to her, spoke and listened, prayed and comforted. The word 'priest' has links with the word 'bridge'. All the Church is involved, but at times we, you and I, are the bridge that links God with his people, and people with their God. Don't let 'orders of ministry' cloud the truth of the ministry of the whole people of God.

In July 1998 my wife and I attended the farewell service for our retiring chairman, Rev F. Ronald Crewes at Wesley's Chapel – it was splendid, and then we dashed down into Kent to share in the weekend celebrations at the first church in my ministry – Hawkhurst Methodist Church was 100 years old! Sitting just behind us was the dear and lovely lady who had been the village baker and our Sunday school superintendent, Miss Gwen Baldock, now 92 years old. She died just a few weeks later, but her faithfulness blessed us and blessed the church. Throughout my ministry I've been blessed by dedicated lay people – members of the 'Laos': the people of God. Keep faithful in your place.

Give me the chance and I'll tell anybody the story of John Wesley, young Jack, being rescued from the fire that destroyed his home, later as a man feeling his heart strangely warmed, preaching in our towns and villages. Give me the chance and I'll tell anybody the stories of the saints who have blessed us on our way. One of them was Victor Chipperfield who, when he married, moved in with his wife and father-in-law. He went with them to worship at the Lenwade Methodist Chapel, Norfolk. There was no one to play the organ, so hymns were sung without music, or read together. One Sunday afternoon after dinner, this hedger and ditcher sat down at his wife's harmonium, opened the tune book to a tune he knew, and, without any musical knowledge, hit key after key through the afternoon until he could play the verse through. Thirty years later he was my church steward and organist at the same church! How can I forget him? Pass on your story of faith, tell others the story of your church, and best of all, tell the stories of Jesus and how you walk with him.

While I'm writing about our doctrines – and the Connexion, unity, ministry and priesthood are all about doctrine – can I quickly say, 'Keep our Methodist emphases!'

I cannot understand why people would go to the stake for the substitutionary theory of the atonement – still only a theory after 2,000 years – but our four 'alls' are a quick and easy summary of our Gospel. All need to be saved. All can be saved. All can know they are saved. All can be saved to the uttermost. Even more briefly, God loves us all, he sent his Son to rescue us, he wants us to come home. Now that's worth living for!

My reading of John Wesley's story, and of our Methodist story since, makes me convinced that we have a charge to keep our emphasis on social responsibility. The Church has never been an ark of safety, hiding from the dangers of the real world. Our work with NCH Action For Children, Methodist Homes, the Relief and Development Fund, Christian Aid, and other organisations, as well as our strong social caring and community development in our city Missions, all give a dimension of God's compassion to our lives and churches. Thank God for Rev Edward Rogers who thrilled me in my earlier days of ministry with his emphasis on Citizenship and Social Responsibility. How sad it is that this part of our Church is now enfeebled and works under the heading 'Public Issues'. Our neighbourhoods, nations and world are crying out for Christian action: 'he has no hands but our hands'! A day at Whitechapel Mission serving breakfasts or teas, or manning the showers and rekitting the homeless men with vests and pants and every other bit of clothing would keep your feet on the ground!

Three years ago I shared in one of the marvellous carol services held at my Bishop's Stortford church. The younger singers paraded us in with the first verse of 'Once in Royal David's City', and, as I neared the front, the orchestra was playing. As I walked past I counted six of our young people playing flutes, apart from those on other instruments. As I waited for the moment to lead the prayer, I realised that all but one of those flute players were going off to university. The question 'How shall we manage without them?' filled my heart. In January, we had a Children and Young People's Concert for NCH Action For Children. One by one, young talents – musical and otherwise – presented themselves on the stage. Amidst the applause, my heart was lifted. I thought, 'We are still God's people, we are still growing, still the Church. The charge, the lamp, is being passed on!'

The best of all is 'God is with us!'

Michael Hayman

MORE THAN WORDS? CHRISTIAN APOLOGETICS FOR A NEW MILLENNIUM

Two broad themes have characterised Christian apologetics: 'defence' and 'persuasion'. These themes have been understood and applied in various ways throughout Christian history. In the earliest centuries some Church leaders were known as 'Apologists', partly because they defined the (true) Faith for those who believed it or wanted to believe it (persuasion), but also because they defended the Faith against those who did not. Then, from around 500 AD, for about a millennium the Western Church ruled. What the Church said 'went', and apologetics became largely the powerful ones stating the case. Apologetics was about defending the status quo and 'persuasion' sadly sometimes became compulsion and coercion. Then came Luther, Calvin and Co. and although the Protestant Reformation changed many things the nature of apologetics remained much the same. Now there was not one but several Churches, each interpreting doctrines for its own people, each spending much time and energy defending its version of the Faith and each attempting to persuade other Christians that it was right.

With the arrival of 'The Enlightenment' and then 'Modernity' (roughly from the 18th century onwards) however, the tight grip of Christianity on Western society was slowly but steadily loosened. The unquestioned right of the Christian Church to define, declare and defend its account of 'life, the universe and everything' was increasingly called into question. After playing 'at home', making the rules and choosing the referee for hundreds of years, the Church increasingly 'played away' and its beliefs were progressively substituted and relegated. Truth, reality and knowledge defined by modernity took the field and won the day year on year. Faced with this development – and for the first time with people who not only dismissed Christian beliefs but also rejected any notion of God – the Church realised that authoritarian apologetics had had their day.

The overall impact of the Enlightenment and modernity upon Christianity is hard to overestimate. Adopting 'critical doubt' as the starting point of any inquiry, question marks were raised over many of the long-held, commonly accepted truths of Christendom. Galileo questioned the traditional way of understanding the universe. Darwin questioned the generally accepted origin of the human race and Karl Marx its fundamental purpose. Freud questioned the nature of religious experience, claiming it to be essentially 'illusory'. These, together with many more thinkers (some of them profoundly Christian believers) changed the way the world, society and individuals were regarded and understood. The dominant role given to reason and the human capacity for rational thought was a common factor. Reason, rather than religion, became regarded by many as the best – even the only – basis on which morality and society could be founded. Science, or more precisely the scientific method of inquiry, replaced theology as the key authority for explaining things; it produced 'facts' and 'proof' rather than (mere) 'beliefs' and 'opinions'. Developments such as these and many others moved Christian faith from the centre of the pitch to a generally respected but nonetheless sidelined place in the real scheme of things.

Christian responses to this fundamental change in how the world was regarded and understood are varied and extremely complex. Nevertheless the twin themes of defence and persuasion remain. Some Christians played ball, using the rules agreed by modernity to try to defend the Faith in an effort to persuade people of its abiding truth. In this way, characteristics of the 'scientific method' were brought to bear on Christianity – its doctrines, scriptures and values – in order to demonstrate its 'reasonableness'. Other Christians 'took their ball home', refusing to play the game by rules which seemed to guarantee their defeat. So faith became increasingly regarded as a private, 'interior' thing, precious and vital to believers, but essentially located in the individual heart, safe from harm. Still other Christians came out fighting, claiming that Christianity alone was 'true' and everything else less so – a sort of 'resiting' of the generally accepted principles of modernity.

Many writers consider that it is during the period of modernity that 'Christian apologetics' came to be recognised as a discipline in its own right. Sometimes referred to as 'evidentialist apologetics', Christian writers defended their faith using the tools and rules determined by modernity, to a greater or lesser extent, and so provided 'evidence' for claims of faith and truth. By this method some fine apologetics appeared in print and continue to do so. Some books take a philosophical line, examining various aspects of Christian faith in relation to the intellectual questions arising from the prevailing culture of the time. Other books begin the other way round, listing 'big questions' such as suffering and evil and suggesting how Christianity 'answers' them. Others take one religious theme, for example the resurrection of Jesus, and look at it from many angles in an attempt to persuade readers that thoughtful, rational people can believe a seemingly implausible idea. Then there is the kind of book written by a Christian who is expert in some non-theological discipline. So, for example, an eminent cosmologist or physicist will relate state-of-the-art thinking in their own field to the Christian Faith with the intention of persuading other specialists and those interested, but less expert, to take more seriously the claims of Christianity than they might otherwise do.

In the long debate with modernity such material has demonstrated repeatedly the remarkable resilience and adaptability of the Christian Faith. Though few would argue that modernity has done Christianity many favours, Christianity has learned to survive, live and, in some respects, even thrive in an inhospitable environment. On the eve of a new millennium some Christians will want to rejoice in the survival of the Faith in the West and recognise the significant role apologetics has played in that. Other Christians will make a more sober judgement, drawing attention to the continuing marginalisation of Christianity and the seemingly inexorable tide of secularisation.

However, increasing numbers of (different and diverse) people – including Christians – are agreed about one thing: we in the West are going through a time of profound cultural change. Terms describing the change such as 'postmodern', 'late modern', or even 'New Age', are less significant than the realisation that our worldview is in a state of flux. It is premature to be precise about the shape of the future, but it is clear than an incarnational religion like Christianity responds to changes in culture. As the canter through Christian history demonstrated earlier it may take time, and not all responses may be equally legitimate, lasting or influential, nevertheless the apologetic task is dynamic rather than static; it changes as the context changes. Given the fact that apologetics is about defence and persuasion, how could it be otherwise?

As we enter a new millennium the nature of Christian apologetics is under review and part of that is the re-appraisal of the apologetics of modernity. In leaning over to speak to the modern world did Christianity too often fall in? And if so, does it matter? Wasn't it all a bit linear and bookish? Didn't modernist apologetics necessarily require 'experts' and thereby de-skill most 'ordinary' Christian people? Aren't non-Christians now coming to see the modernist method of 'proof' as too limiting? As one scholar put it, 'The human spirit cannot live permanently with the form of rationality which has no answer to the question "why?"'

It would be short-sighted in the extreme to suggest that reason and empirical logic have no place in the apologetics of the 21st century. Reason is not contrary to faith even though faith is not wholly explained by reason. Perhaps the very fact that this is accepted and appreciated today more than for a long time past is in part due to Christian apologetics banging the drum? Also, to state that Christianity cannot be reduced to modernist reason is a very different thing to suggesting that it is – or should be – irrational.

Christianity cannot share in the chaotic incoherence of some contemporary spiritualities. To do so is a recipe for disaster because no part of Christian discipleship ignores the use of the mind, and proper use of the mind glorifies God. In fact, over huge areas of human life in the West there is little to suggest that empirical reason is anything other than alive and well. Sciences, technologies, biologies, much of medicine, indeed most of the items on *Tomorrow's World* and other TV programmes like it make the case. Though modernity is not the favoured worldview of the *X-Files* or most computer games, the ability to watch or play is firmly indebted to its methodology. So whatever else is needed for a new millennium it is not a simple ditching of all reason, which will remain an essential factor in presenting Christianity as a plausible and therefore possible choice to make. We may no longer feel constrained to make our case by the narrowest rules of modernity but the proper use of human reason and intellect cannot be abandoned.

Yet there is something else needed – apologetics that are both/and rather than either/or – apologetics of the head *and* . . . Overall the apologetics of modernity are probably better at defence than persuasion. As Alister McGrath puts it: 'Traditional apologetics has sought to commend Christianity, without asking why it is that so many people are not Christians.' The present cultural shift encourages Christians to realise that apologetics are required to be receptor-friendly, responsive rather than propositional, and that this instantly moves us into a both/and mode. To ask the question 'What prevents people becoming Christian?' is (whatever else it is) an apologetics question. Thoroughly researched answers to this type of question suggest there are a number of factors involved. A British survey by the Christian Research Association, as recently as 1998, claimed that for 40 per cent of men and 50 per cent of women surveyed, suffering was a major barrier to faith. But there were other significant barriers. For over a third of women the issue of 'marginalisation' was a key barrier to Christian faith.

Similarly, a few years ago Robert Kachur discovered among young Americans in Ivy League universities that the top reasons for rejecting Christianity were not, as was expected, intellectual reasons, but were that Christians were regarded as hypocrites and 'too exclusive'. George Hunter III has spent a lifetime researching such questions in both the US and the UK and observes that very few people are won to Christian faith by purely academic apologetics or, just as significantly, prevented from finding faith by purely academic questions. It appears that for a large majority of Western people to be loved, listened to, and valued is at least as important as answering the 'big questions'.

This understanding of apologetics widens the nature of the task from narrow modernist definitions and it also opens up the task to the whole people of God. Twenty-first century Christianity needs the expert Christian physicist, the theologian and the philosopher. But it also needs 'ordinary' church congregations and individual Christians living out the Christian life in such a way that charges of exclusivism, superiority and hypocrisy are countered by experiences of grace and profound, open spirituality. Such 'head and heart' apologetics relates to young and old alike. As Lesslie Newbigin put it: 'The only hermeneutic of the Gospel is a congregation of men and women who believe it and live by it.' This is apologetics beyond books and literacy in a contemporary culture that in many respects is becoming increasingly 'oral' and relational. The contemporary cultural context is new and demanding; apologetics understood in this way is not.

In the early, heady centuries of Christianity, the way Christians lived and died were key factors in the persuasive defence of faith. But we can go even further back, to Jesus himself. His model of presence, grace and humility, of living among, of listening and teaching (in parables?) seems to me to be a crucial one for apologetics as we enter the new millennium. His call to 'Follow me' is not a leap in the dark but an act of faith, and between the two is the world of difference.

Martyn Atkins

DEVELOPING PARTNERSHIPS – MEETING YOU WHERE YOU ARE

As George Whitefield's 'field preaching' took off in the 1730s, he realised that this successful but novel ministry was reaching people the established Church could never encounter. But he was under great pressure to go to America, so, with difficulty, persuaded his friend John Wesley to take on this work. Wesley, a stiff High Church Anglican clergyman, was not enthusiastic about being at the mercy of a ragtag crowd of dirty workers, and was scared stiff, believing that he was risking his life. But he was under divine constraint. In April 1739 his diary records that he 'submitted to be more vile' and he began by preaching to miners in Bristol and then Kingswood. He realised at once that he was preaching to people who would never go to church, but who were hungry for the message and astonishingly responsive. Wesley was taking the Gospel to them on their own ground, and they accepted him and his words gladly.

This chapter will look at the three strands of the work of the Methodist Relief and Development Fund (MRDF) – meeting need through development, changing lifestyles through development education, and tackling structural injustice. To begin a chapter on the work of MRDF with this story about our

Wesleyan heritage might seem a little odd. But it reflects the kind of development and development education we are working on in our late 20th century context. It's a context which has seen dramatic change in the 50 years that MRDF has existed,[1] change in the world and in our own Church. In the UK we are constantly told that numbers are falling. But the international scene, in which MRDF works, tells the story of a worldwide Methodist Church that is growing and has become an influential player in many countries.

MRDF's development policy reflects Wesley's realisation that taking the Gospel to people on their own territory is a powerful way of operating. Our development is about going to people on their terms. It's about them setting the agenda, not about us imposing our ideas of what we think is good for them – responding to a need, not creating one. It's about building partnerships on the basis that both partners have something of equal value to contribute. This concept of partnership is centred on some core ideas:

1.   We aim to work with indigenous organisations, set up by local people for local people. They are the ones who know what the local needs are, and how best to meet them in their context.

2.   MRDF partners are typically small, non-governmental organisations (NGOs) and charities. We have found that such groups tend to be very dynamic and highly motivated, and our grant of between £5,000 and £10,000 is used by them in creative and effective ways. A very happy moment for MRDF is when a small organisation we've been funding for many years grows beyond our capacity and is able to attract bigger donors. MRDF has supported Nijera Shikhi, a literacy movement in Bangladesh, since 1994. Their success in reaching

illiterates has been so phenomenal that they have now attracted funding from governments and Christian Aid. From MRDF's point of view, this is the successful realisation of our kind of development!

3. Our partners are the ones who set the agenda, and this may mean changing the use of a grant from what was originally stated, or topping it up if necessary. In Sri Lanka, the Seva Sevana Community Development Programme wanted to train local women in sewing skills, and applied to us for a grant to buy their own sewing machines. After it had been allocated, they realised that the women could be trained at the local Singer factory instead. So they asked if they could use the grant to build a kitchen at the church instead, in order to improve another part of the programme, its day-care facilities. This was still an integral part of the programme, and in line with MRDF policy, so it was agreed straightaway.

4. We look at development in the long term, and allocate many grants on a three-year basis. Even after this, we are happy to stick with partners if they still need our support, or help them move on. The Jajarkot Permaculture Programme in Nepal has been encouraging small-scale organic farming amongst remote villages for 10 years, to which MRDF has contributed from the beginning.

5. Our partners do not have to be Methodist – they don't even have to be Christian. We work with Muslims in Croatia, mixed religious groups in Israel, and secular organisations all over the world. The World Church supports other Methodist Conferences around the world, and it is right that we should work with our Methodist brothers and sisters where possible. MRDF fulfils another part of the mission of the Methodist Church, taking its cue from the story of

the sheep and the goats in Matthew 25 – to meet need, wherever it is.

MRDF has historically funded a lot of work in the field of agroforestry, water and literacy. But the above core ideas are crucial to the application of any agency, regardless of its sphere of work.

There is a second strand to MRDF's work – development education (DE). DE has played a part in Methodism for many years, dating back to the work of the Division of Social Responsibility in the 1950s. This approach to DE is also unique among the Churches; although they work on DE issues, MRDF employs a Development Education Officer, and this is not reflected in any other denomination. Methodism recognises the need to act here as well as in the developing world, and stands out historically and in the present climate in this respect.

MRDF's DE work reflects Wesley's model of taking issues to people on their terms. In this case, the people are the Methodist people of Britain and Ireland, and the issue is the interdependency of the developed and developing world in the late 20th century. We live in a global society, where simple lifestyle choices that you and I make matter. From the everyday business of coffee, bananas and trainers, to insurance, investments and even going on holiday, the decisions we take impact on people living in developing countries, on their economies, jobs and therefore their lives.[2] DE raises awareness about these decisions, and the links they create between our lives and the lives of people in the developing world. MRDF uses stories and examples from the projects it funds to bring those links to the attention of Methodists in an accessible but challenging format. It raises awareness about choices Methodists can make, and gives them the option to campaign for political change as well.

Crucially, though, MRDF links DE with the Bible. In fact, our model of storytelling to convey meaning and make links has a good scriptural basis; the Gospels echo with Jesus' parables, which brought home the truth about God's love to first century people. MRDF grounds its DE work in the Bible, and starts by making links between its faith and development work. Through its worship material, it aims to bring development issues to the centre of the Church's worshipping life, and to inspire Methodists to make practical lifestyle choices as a direct result of the links they have made. Often, a developing world perspective can illuminate biblical stories or truths. It's not until you have seen a flock of sheep – or are they goats? – in India or Palestine or Peru that you realise that sheep and goats look very similar in the developing world, and cannot easily be distinguished in the way they are here. It puts the story of the sheep and the goats (Matthew 25) in a whole new light!

So where is MRDF heading as we turn to the new millennium? We aim at a continual improvement of our development practice, and at maintaining the centrality of our work within the mission of the Methodist Church. We are calling the millennium 'A Time To Plant' (Ecclesiastes 3: 1-2), and raising money to continue valuable tree planting work through our Millennium Trees Fund.[3] But in the late 20th century, the struggle for social justice is complicated, and another strand of action needs to be added to the two we have already discussed. The world is structured around certain philosophies and institutions, and few of them work to the advantage of the world's poor. Feeding the hungry and buying fairly-traded coffee matter, but our third strand of action involves tackling the bigger, structural issues, such as global finance and economics.

Were you one of the 70,000 people who went to the G8 summit in Birmingham on 16 May 1997 to show support for the Jubilee 2000 campaign? This movement aims to tackle one of the major contributors to poverty – third world debt – by cancelling the unpayable debt of the world's poorest countries by 2000 under a fair and transparent process. The campaign originated within the Churches and has received strong support from them, but now it spans all sectors of society, religion, class and age. It has caught the imagination of this country, and debt as an issue has moved rapidly up the international agenda as the campaign spreads across the world. MRDF supports Jubilee 2000 financially, to pay for staff costs in its London office, and also practically by resourcing local Methodists and the Methodist press. The proceeds from this book will also go to support the campaign. In today's world, no one strand of action will do – all three have a vital part to play.

Jubilee 2000 is a big movement for social justice that has swept the nation and the world – and that brings us back to where we started, to our Methodist heritage. Wesley's legacy was a Church plugged into issues of social justice. This part of the Church that Wesley founded is rooted in our Methodist tradition, but has its eyes firmly on the future, and the continued needs of the poor. We hope that you will continue to support our work in the years to come. By doing so, you will affirm the place of the struggle for justice for the world's poor at the heart of 21st century Methodism.

Caro Ayres

Notes
1. The Methodist Relief Fund (MRF) started its work in 1945, providing food parcels for people in Germany after the second world war. It then expanded to meet other developing country needs. In the 1970s, the World Development Fund (WDF) was formed, to tackle the causes of poverty and underdevelopment as well as the effects. Some aspects of its work were considered 'non-charitable' by the Inland Revenue; in 1981 the non-charitable World Development Action Fund (WDAF) was established to take on the political aspect of this work. The MRF and the WDF were merged in 1985 to create the Methodist Relief and Development Fund (MRDF), while the WDAF remained distinct from MRDF but linked to it, in the conviction of the importance of the struggle for justice and our responsibility for that.

2. See *The Good Life Guide,* published by the World Development Movement (1998), 25, Beehive Place, London, SW9 7QR, 0171 737 6215 for more information.

3. If you'd like to take part in this campaign, please call Caro Ayres on 0171 222 8010 for your free resources pack.

INTERNATIONAL AND INTERDEPENDENT

Every member of the Methodist Church is a member of the Methodist Missionary Society – it is a matter of discipleship, not of interest or obligation.

The history of the Methodist Missionary Society is an honourable one and those who read or hear the stories of individual and family courage and perseverance in the face of danger and hardship cannot fail to be moved by such commitment and determination. In many countries the Methodist Missionary Society bought land, educated children and adults, established hospitals, clinics and village health centres. They built churches and manses and engaged in evangelism, establishing new churches and ordaining ministers. John Wesley's 'the world is my parish' may not have been a thought-out policy when he uttered it, but it became one of the rallying calls of the Church which had the confidence to go into all the world to preach, teach, baptise and heal. And individuals, churches and circuits raised money by various means in order to support the work which was being done, responding to the wonderful stories which flowed back to the 'home country' and 'Mother Church'.

In my childhood I was thrilled by the black and white filmstrip of 'Pygmies in Africa', embarrassed by the returned missionary who tied me up in a sari and confused by the thought of putting rice (which was a pudding to me) on the same plate as stew! This seems so far from the experience of many people today. Overseas does not have the same mystery and sense of adventure it once had. Ease of overseas travel, where many people holiday in far-away places, and the cultural diversity which exists in most towns and cities of Britain today have brought more understanding of different ways of life. Into our homes come the daily pictures of life lived in other places, many of those images of famine, poverty and desperate need, but also those of corruption, wealth and conflict.

The churches established by the early missionaries have one by one become autonomous Churches with their own ethos and identity, governed by their own Conferences and adopting policies which may not always coincide with those of the British Church. The rich relationship with Britain is retained in most cases, but relationships are also entered into with other Churches and agencies.

We are as committed as we ever were to our understanding of one family of God, joint heirs of creation and salvation, but I suggest that our role within this world society is a changing one. There has always been the understanding of two main calls within the missionary endeavour; one the 'go and tell' of the Gospel imperative, the other the 'come over and help us' once the vision has been shared. The balance has swung further towards the invitation to mutual sharing in the mission of Christ, and the 'come over' cry is as relevant in Britain as in Africa.

At a consultation within the World Church Office we questioned whether the word 'partner' adequately describes the essential relationship we have with

Churches round the world. It was felt to be too restrictive a word for the inclusive and open-ended relationships which we try to foster. We suggested that the word 'companions' reflects better the nature of our journey in faith together, having as it does the sense of 'with bread' of both resource sharing and communion in the Body of Christ.

One of the ways we are seeking to create the means of sharing ideas and understandings of the Gospel is in the consultations we now arrange annually with representatives of overseas Churches who are invited to attend the British Conference. In June 1998 Bishop Aldo Etchegoyen of the Methodist Church in Argentina led the thinking about the nature of our relationships within world Methodism. He said, 'We must come to a moment when we will not be autonomous Churches seeking to express connectionality, but connectional Churches on an equal footing. This by no means signifies a leap backwards into the past, but rather a leap forward in search of a new situation in which we can truly express our genuine connectionality in service of life, in maturity and in coherence with the Gospel. A connectionality which surges up from our national roots is enriched by the diversity of world Methodism in the setting of the great ecumenical family.'

Today our sharing is expressed in a number of different ways. The most precious and cherished partnership is in the exchange of personnel. The word 'missionary' has given way to the use of the term 'mission partner'. This reflects the nature of the partnership into which we enter. Today the mission partner is not always involved directly in evangelism or church building but can be an agriculturist, an engineer, a disability advisor, a teacher, nurse or doctor. The selection and training process ensures that people are well-prepared for the changes in culture and living conditions which will be experienced. The task is always one which has been requested by the overseas Church and much consultation takes place before an appointment is made by the Methodist Council to the work.

Similar consultations take place when the mission partner is coming to Britain in order to assist in mission here. Overseas Churches release some of their best ministers to serve in circuit ministry, the connexional team or theological college through the World Church in Britain Partnership programme. They also send ministers and lay people through the Mission Live programme in order to encourage and educate churches and circuits to catch the vision of the World Church family.

The Scholarship Programme offers opportunities for people to take further courses to equip them better for leadership in their own church. Many students come to Britain to be trained in a variety of ways, but often today churches prefer to send students to a neighbouring country which offers an appropriate course, so one will go from Zimbabwe to South Africa, or from Myanmar to Singapore. The students who come to Britain enjoy the contacts made with Methodists who offer hospitality and many rich friendships begin in this way.

Methodist people are still very generous in giving money to be used in World Church projects. Significant sums are given through the World Church Office to Churches overseas in general grants to be spent according to the priorities set by them. Special grants are made throughout the year whenever there are special needs identified or crises which occur. It is largely the responsibility of the four World Church Secretaries to liase with Church leaders about the grants which are made; there has to be great sensitivity to enable the giving of money to enrich our relationship rather than to allow it to become one of dependency or unhealthy patronage.

The Methodist Relief and Development Funds are another avenue by which Methodists in Britain can contribute towards relieving the needs of people in other places. The provision of clean water, tree planting, new methods of agriculture and forestry, sustainable economies and environmental advice enables communities in many areas to develop.

There is a great sense of satisfaction in being united in mission with others from around the world. However, great care has to be taken that in sharing in mission there is a reciprocal relationship. A Church leader in Pakistan, addressing a group of mission agencies, said, 'You meet together discussing us and our needs, but still hold your moneybags and agendas close to your chests . . . It gives us the feeling that each one of you wants to hold on to that power which gives you the privilege of being the donor in your relationship with us.' There is much we need to receive from the insights and experiences of others. After all, the growth in the Church is being experienced in these days in many places while the Methodist Church in Britain is losing members. The interdependent quality of our relationships will be increasingly the pattern for the future.

We are having to learn again the appropriate ways of encouraging participation in the World Church. The Church has come to our doorsteps in its international dimension. It is worth noting here that it is not only the hospitality the churches offer Christians from other countries with which the Church is concerned. Many Methodists are involved with the policies and practices of the government agencies with regard to asylum seekers and refugees. Campaigning for justice and human rights, seeking freedom from unpayable debts and seeking to promote peacemaking are often the most effective ways of expressing a sense of international understanding and commitment.

A rich diversity of culture and faith is present in our communities and it is no longer helpful to try to differentiate between home and overseas (once foreign!) mission. The same understanding of culture difference is as needed in Bradford as it is in Bombay. Christianity is almost becoming the minority faith within British secular society as it is in other places and the ways which have proved to be useful in addressing the unchurched need to be developed here.

One of the ways in which the Methodist Church is responding to this new dimension is to enter into a programme of exchange and education intended to develop formation in world mission. It is hoped that soon every candidate for ministry, both presbyteral and diaconal, will be offered the opportunity to spend part of their training for ministry in a different cultural setting and that programmes will be arranged which will offer lay people more opportunities for exchange experiences. New courses of study will open up creative ways of using insights gained from other experiences to stimulate a sense of participation in the great world community of faith.

That world community is celebrated as Methodists within the World Methodist Council and we are aware of an increasing need to consult with our cousins in the United Methodist Church. In February 2000 there will be a consultation for those countries in which both aspects of Methodism have partnership links and this may lead to other avenues of co-operation. The World Methodist Conference meets in Brighton in 2001. We also celebrate our place in many ecumenical alliances which increase immeasurably our links across the continents.

The future? Increasingly rapid change makes it hard to predict where our future priorities will lie. There seems to be no end to the conflicts which rack people, or to the violence, greed and corruption which bedevil any hope of eradicating poverty or narrowing the gap between rich and poor.

But gradually the antagonism between some churches and communities is being replaced with the desire for co-operation and often in history it has been the sense of desperation which has sent people looking for God. We continue to seek ways of building bridges and becoming communities of hope. We may not have the same dominant role, but we have not been released from the responsibility to take our place among God's people and proclaim his power and his grace.

Kathleen Richardson

ELDERS NOT OLDIES

'Eventide Homes – the Conference appoints the following Committee to explore the possibility of establishing a Home or Homes for Aged Methodists . . .' Thus reads a minute of the Methodist Conference of 1942. Amongst those nominated was the Rev Walter Hall who was appointed Convenor. Rightly so, since this modest development was the fruit of Walter Hall's concern that there should be some alternative to the notorious 'Workhouse' for poor elderly church members such as those belonging to his congregation in Tottenham at that time.

Through God's good providence it turned out to be a committee that was more than just a talking shop. By the next Conference it reported that exhaustive enquiries had been made into the need amongst Methodists and the lack of adequate provision by charities, public authorities, voluntary organisations and the churches. Amongst the recommendations adopted was the following: 'While the needs of Methodists should have priority in Methodist Homes, others would be welcomed as accommodation permitted.' Methodist Homes has never been exclusive. Residents were 'usually' to be aged 60 or more, a far cry from the average age of almost 90 of new residents on the eve of the new millennium. It is surely a cause for wonder that the Birmingham Conference should have entertained such vision and made such positive decisions as the bombs of the second world war were falling there and on other British cities.

So Methodist Homes for the Aged was born. At the 1945 Conference an appeal was made to the Methodist Connexion to raise £50,000 so that premises might be purchased, adapted and furnished. New buildings were not in the picture at this early stage. Despite some reservations, this target figure was in fact increased to £60,000 in response to a generous challenge offer from the Joseph Rank Benevolent Trust. By the summer of 1945 the first home, 'Ryelands' at Wallington in Surrey was opened, closely followed by homes at Harrogate, Tankerton, Ilkley, Liverpool, Bognor Regis and Hathersage. Such rapid expansion was facilitated by the generosity of such Methodist philanthropists as Hilda Bartlett Lang, daughter of Joseph Rank and the first treasurer of the organisation, and Sir George Martin, who became the first chairman. The inspirational Flower Fund, which encouraged donations in lieu of flowers in memory of those who died, helped to raise both the profile of MHA and the funds required, especially following its espousal by Margaret Harwood in her *Methodist Recorder* column.

The story of Methodist Homes' first 30 years is well told by the late Cyril Davey in his book *Home from Home*. He records that by 1976 there was a total of 34 homes. It has to be said that the great majority of residents were Methodists, female, in good health and able to meet the modest fees, for the homes were not in those early days staffed or equipped to cope with high dependency. From the outset, with the exception of 'Trembaths' at Letchworth which is dual-registered as both a nursing and a residential home, Methodist Homes has favoured the more 'family' ethos of the latter over against the medical model of the former. They were, however, innovative in a number of ways. Generously proportioned single room accommodation has always been the norm, with double room facilities for couples. Incoming residents were (and still are) encouraged to bring their own furniture and personal belongings so that their room would remain 'home' for them. Each home has always had the services of a part-time chaplain who is usually a minister on the staff of a local circuit. Until 1994 Methodist lay people shouldered much of the management responsibility through the local home committees and by their involvement and support have always enhanced the community life of each home.

With the passing of the years Methodist Homes also adapted to the changing needs of older people and so did not become ossified in a single model of care. Most older people wish to remain independent and stay in their own homes if possible until the end of their lives. They wish to retain 'their own front door'. From the mid-1970s Methodist Homes therefore began to build sheltered housing schemes, mostly accommodating similar numbers to the residential homes and each with their chaplain and committee. Sheltered housing schemes are looked after by wardens (since re-named 'scheme managers') who provide a caring presence and ensure the provision of support services when required. In 1977 Methodist Homes Housing Association was formed in order to take advantage of the financial support offered by the government-appointed Housing Corporation, and this greatly facilitated the spread of sheltered housing provision.

A decade later the Live at Home initiative was launched to enhance the quality of life of older people living on their own through the befriending, encouragement and support of volunteers. Responsive to the perceived needs of their locality, the

40 or so schemes have all evolved differently, some developing drop-in facilities and lunch clubs, many giving opportunities for social activities and outings, a few offering specific services such as gardening or carer relief. However, Live at Home schemes do not fulfil functions that properly belong to the statutory services. All have part-time paid co-ordinators and are heavily dependent on volunteers recruited from the churches and the wider community.

At about the same time as the Live at Home initiative began, the opportunity arose to set up a specialist dementia care residential home at Newport Pagnell in partnership with Buckinghamshire Social Services and the Area Health Authority. Alzheimer's disease and other forms of dementia currently affect one in five of all people over 80 years of age, and there is at present no cure. However, a person's well-being can be improved and sustained through sensitive person-centred care. 'Westbury' developed a considerable reputation and became an invaluable training resource for care staff from other Methodist homes. In the late 1990s two further dedicated homes have been built, at Ellesmere Port and Stoke-on-Trent. At some other homes dementia care wings are being added to obviate the need for residents to have to move and thus compound the confusion that is part of this distressing illness.

Increasing physical and mental frailty has become an inexorable fact of life for Methodist Homes since the outworking of the 1990 NHS and Community Care Act, which has meant that older people can receive Social Services support to enter residential care only when their needs are assessed as requiring this. People with dementia are amongst the most marginalised in our society, and Methodist Homes has looked upon its work in this area as being a response to John Wesley's injunction to the Methodist people: 'Go not to those who need you but to those who need you most.'

Thus, at the end of the second millennium, Methodist Homes finds itself employing almost 2,000 staff, many of whom work part-time, rejoicing in the priceless support of over 4,000 volunteers, and caring for some 1,300 residents, 800 tenants in sheltered housing and almost 3,000 members of Live at Home schemes. The annual turnover is £27 million and the charitable income £5 million, much of which comes directly or indirectly from the Methodist people, not least through legacies and Methodist Homes Sunday collections. Most important of all are the prayers of all who support Methodist Homes. Such a committed and sustained response is seen as an endorsement of Walter Hall's original vision and the way in which Methodist Homes has sought to fulfil it.

And what of the future? In 1994 Methodist Homes underwent an organisational review to equip it better to respond to the needs of post-community care British society. After four more years' experience and the appointment of a new Chief Executive to step into the shoes of David Wigley, who had led the organisation through 15 eventful years, the restructuring was taken further as a consequence of a wide-ranging 'Future Directions' consultative process which identified three primary goals to take the organisation into the new millennium.

In Methodist parlance, these primary goals represent a commitment to good stewardship, mission and the spiritual dimension of life. Thus Methodist Homes is committed to reviewing all the existing locations where it works in order to develop a greater range of services, to developing strategies and finding appropriate partners to establish new services in more deprived areas of society, and to setting up a spirituality centre through which the spiritual aspects of ageing can be more intensively addressed for the benefit not just of the organisation but of the Church and the wider community. These goals cannot be achieved without the understanding and continued support of the Methodist people.

Methodist Homes offers 'a model of mutual consultancy' to the Methodist Church. Churches and individual Christians have invaluable experience both of ageing and its spirituality and of caring for older people. Methodist Homes has its own expertise to offer. The Christian constituency needs to make its voice heard in the political debates about the implications of an ageing population. Most of all, older people need to be seen not as 'oldies' to be done-good-to but as respected elders with a vital contribution to make to the well-being of church and society. The challenge is such that Methodist Homes and the Church will need each other as never before!

Methodist Homes, whilst it is the largest Christian-based organisation caring for older people in Britain, obviously cannot be all things to all people. Priorities will need to be established and resources handled with proper stewardship. Financial and political realities will always have to be taken into account. However, with the continued support and partnership of the Methodist people, Methodist Homes is determined to be as committed and innovative in its care as ever as it faces the challenges of the new millennium. In the economy of God's kingdom, vision and faith have always counted for much more than the always limited material and human resources. This is as true today as it was when Methodist Homes was founded nearly 60 years ago, or indeed 2,000 years ago.

Albert Jewell

'IT'S OF LITTLE CONCERN'

In 1869 a young Methodist minister, Thomas Bowman Stephenson, arrived in London to take up his new appointment in the Lambeth Circuit. Stephenson's charge was the chapel in Waterloo Road. The bridge was only a hundred yards away, linking Lambeth with the finery of The Strand for the charge of a halfpenny bridge toll. In contrast, the 'New Cut', not far from the chapel and Stephenson's manse, was a notorious area marked by poverty and crime.

In Lambeth, children's lives were scarred by poverty. Many of them roamed the streets shoeless, dirty and with the look of hunger in their eyes. Stephenson suspected that many of them were completely homeless. Moved by compassion and anger at the plight of children who, to many, 'were of little concern', Stephenson said, 'Here were my poor little brothers and sisters, sold to Hunger and the Devil. How could I be free of their blood if I could not try to save some of them? I began to feel my time had come.'

We may be lulled into thinking that poverty in Britain is history but, sadly, this isn't so. In late Victorian society, 28 per cent of the population were 'destitute'. Today, three million of the 12 million dependent children in Britain lead lives that are scarred by poverty and the experience of social exclusion. Standards, of course, change and poverty now is not the same as in Victorian times. Historical perspective, however, is no consolation to the child or young person who is hungry and homeless or neglected and abused. In Britain today the names of 35,000 children are held on Child Protection registers though the incidence of child abuse is probably much greater than these figures suggest.

Together with two Methodist friends, Alfred Mager and Frances Horner, Stephenson began the renovation of a disused stable in Church Street, and the first two boys – Fred and George – were admitted on 9th July 1869. The name chosen – 'The Children's Home' – reflected Stephenson's far-sighted commitment to a family system of child care. 'We do not desire to establish an institution,' Stephenson said and, for him, the choice of the word 'Home' signalled his commitment to providing innovative ways of meeting children's needs that were a radical alternative to the workhouse. He wanted to provide for the disadvantaged the quality of love and care that advantaged children experienced in any decent and caring family. In the age of the workhouse and *Oliver Twist*, this was a radical step. Stephenson was also a great campaigner, committed to challenging the Church and wider society about their responsibility to those who were so often regarded as 'of little concern'.

A pamphlet published at the very beginning of the work, in July 1869, began to circulate widely and attracted new support and wider interest. On the front page, the objective of 'The Home' was set out – 'To rescue children who, through the death or vice or extreme poverty of parents, are in danger of falling into criminal ways'.

Stephenson met opposition even from within the Church. There were those who protested about the 'bad characters' he was admitting to the Home. The poor were often blamed for their own misfortunes and there were calls for savage punishments to keep the 'dangerous classes' in order. In *The Children's Advocate*, published in September 1874, Stephenson wrote, 'There are no utterly friendless children under God's heaven. Earthly friends may have forgotten them or forsaken them . . . but God watches over every child.'

The emphasis on the importance of professional training was one of Stephenson's great contributions to the development of child care in the UK. 'It is a huge mistake,' he said, 'to suppose that anybody who can wash a child's face or sew a button upon a child's dress is fit for such work as ours.' The training policy radically elevated the status of those caring for children and assured the success of 'The Children's Home'.

During the inter-war years, the 'National Children's Home', as it was then known, campaigned for the legal recognition of adoption, becoming an adoption agency itself in 1926. Later, it influenced the 1948 Children Act, which paved the way for adoption to become the leading child care strategy. The changing social climate brought a huge increase in placements – principally of 'illegitimate' babies – and in peak years the National Children's Home was finding families for more than 300 infants a year.

The roots of modern practice can be seen right from the beginning. Even in the 1880s siblings were placed together and difficult children were found families. From the 1920s, children were carefully matched with adoptive families and encouraged to think well of their birth parents. In 1935 a Children's Charter was published, which stated that children had: 'the right to be born in love and honour . . . in an environment that will provide for normal development . . . the right to love, protection, care . . . the right to liberty and justice . . . and to be safeguarded from neglect, abuse, cruelty, exploitation . . . the right to be treated with the regard due to a child of God'. The spirit and the letter of this statement prefigures today's United Nations' Declaration on the Rights of the Child.

NCH Action For Children continues its work in the tradition established by Thomas Bowman Stephenson. It is now one of Britain's leading child care charities and an influential campaigner for social justice for children, young people and their families.

The tradition within Methodism of standing alongside the most vulnerable and marginalised members of society, often regarded as 'of little concern', informs the purpose and values at the heart of NCH Action For Children's mission to bring a better quality of life to the most vulnerable children.

Stephenson believed that greater social progress, better education and a wider sense of social responsibility would ensure the well-being and security of all children. Sadly, that vision is yet to be realised. In pursuit of this goal, NCH Action For Children today provides help for more than 36,000 children, young people and their families in over 370 projects nationwide. The diverse range of services covers:

- families with young children in need
- communities in need
- children/young people with disabilities or special needs
- children/young people caring for adults/siblings
- children needing families
- children/adults affected by sexual abuse

- children/young people leaving care and/or at risk of homelessness
- children/young people requiring residential services, including education
- young people/families needing advice or counselling
- children/young people who have offended/involved in the criminal justice system
- research/evaluation and consultancy

It was the problem of homelessness, and all the problems that attend it, that inspired the foundation of the organisation. Now, generations later, the battle is to be fought today. A range of compelling research, including our own, indicates that the number of homeless young people has increased significantly in recent years. In London alone, there are estimated to be almost 80,000 young people, some as young as 16, either sleeping rough or living in unsuitable, short-term accommodation. Research suggests that between a third and half of all homeless young people are those whose childhoods have been spent in care. Also, a large percentage of homeless young people are running away from situations of domestic violence or abuse.

In February 1997, the House our Youth 2000 Campaign was launched, aimed at raising public awareness about the serious problem of youth homelessness in Britain. In addition, NCH Action For Children agreed a five-year leaving care and young homeless initiative, which commits the organisation to allocating over £3 million from voluntary income to develop urgently needed services to support young people leaving care and those threatened with homelessness. Other community-based projects can also help to prevent breakdown in families with adolescents.

NCH Action For Children believes that youth homelessness is not inevitable, is relatively recent in terms of its current scale, and could be solved by the right mix of national and local policies. Against the background of our history and current role as the largest national provider of services to young homeless people and care leavers, it is an appropriate task for the organisation to work with others to campaign for an end to youth homelessness. Indeed, it is part of the mission established by Thomas Bowman Stephenson and 'a charge' that we carry forward today.

NCH Action For Children remains a Christian-based organisation, accountable to the Methodist Conference. Christian-based social care has roots in a number of traditions within the life of the Church and, consequently, there are a variety of examples of such social care. NCH Action For Children represents those working on a 'partnership basis'.

Partnership will usually be with statutory agencies but also with some voluntary organisations. Employment policy will focus on employing those best equipped to provide a quality service, who may not necessarily be Christians but who share the aims and objectives of the organisation. The evolution of such partnerships has been influenced by developments in the profession of social work, changes in society and the proper requirements of legislation, especially in relation to providing for the needs of children.

It is crucial that the work is owned and affirmed by the Church as an expression of the implications of the Gospel and the vision of a caring society. In an increasingly diverse and multi-faith society, it is important that the Church, through its agencies of social care, is willing to enter into genuine partnership. This does not mean sacrificing or watering down our beliefs but represents a willingness to explore what mutuality means. Then shared concerns can lead, in partnership with others, towards creating a just and caring society.

It is sometimes an uncomfortable position because seriously entering into equal partnership with others means relinquishing the right to have total control. The partnership model is challenging because differences have to be positively acknowledged and faced. The opportunities, however, are considerable and enable the Church to influence debates about social policy and to offer critical, ethical and theological reflection around the issues facing society and human relationships.

The work of NCH Action For Children can be interpreted as part of the Church's healing ministry – the healing of broken relationships; the healing of trauma in a sexually abused child; the discovery of self-worth in the life of a young person leaving care and faced with the daunting task of building an independent life. In many respects, the work of caring agencies is exactly the kind of work which scripture understands as the work of salvation; of healing; of promoting justice and righteousness. It is the work of Christ, and the work to which Christ calls his followers.

In 1993, the Methodist Conference endorsed this statement: 'The focal points of the Church's concern are God and the world. It exists only for the sake of the kingdom, where God's love directs all things.'[1]

The work undertaken by NCH Action For Children as the child care charity of the Methodist Church reflects that vision of 'the kingdom' which is at the heart of the ministry of Jesus, who worked to secure wholeness and freedom as a gift for all God's children. In the teaching of Jesus, who died for all, there is an inclusive picture of 'the kingdom' in which the poor, the homeless and the marginalised have a special place and in which God's generous love reaches out like that of a loving parent to meet the needs of all his children.

Setbacks and opposition were not uncommon experiences in the early days for Stephenson and his two supporters but, as he said, 'We believed God's hand was in the enterprise from the moment we commenced it.' The remarkable developments over the years and the continuing place NCH Action For Children has within the Methodist family is a tribute to Stephenson's vision and a pointer to God's continuing presence in this crucial enterprise of care.

Bill Lynn

Notes
1. Taken from the 'Shared Theological Statement' contained in the report of the President's Council to Conference.

FAITH IN OURSELVES

I want to tell you a story. It happened a long time ago, but it is still so fresh in my mind it seems it was only yesterday; strange isn't it, I can hardly remember what I had for breakfast yesterday, but *this* day – what a day it was!

We had this friend, you see. Who's 'we', you may ask? There were four of us who had met at the local Job Centre, all of us in our early fifties. We were what you might call 'middle management' men, and each had been the subject of what I think is called 'downsizing' in the jargon of modern economics. I said four, but in fact there were five of us. Jim, he came into the Centre in a wheelchair, for he had been injured at work and although he had a fine mind, nobody had given him an interview for years.

You have to wait an awfully long time at those places, so the five of us got into conversation and afterwards we went for a drink together. That's when it all started and we pledged we would stay in touch, and we did, we did all manner of things together. Well, you can when you have all the time in the world. I won't bore you with all the ups and downs of the group, except to say some of us had short spells of employment, but Jim never managed to get even one interview and he sank deeper and deeper into despondency and worthlessness – it used to worry us all.

Back to this particular day. We'd heard that this carpenter, who'd made quite a reputation for himself as a preacher and healer, was back in town. He'd been on a mission and had returned, and not only him; a large crowd had followed him back home. The four of us resolved that somehow we had to get him to meet Jim. So we set out. It was a beautiful morning and all we had to do was follow the crowd. We talked excitedly about the things we had heard about this Jesus and what he might do for Jim – but when we arrived at the house, we couldn't get anywhere near it. There were hundreds and hundreds of people crowded round the gate and the path.

But as Yorkshire men we were not going to be thwarted without having a go. I took charge of the wheelchair and its occupant and in my most authoritative way loudly said, 'Excuse me – do you mind?' and told the others to keep close. (They always said you could still see, all these years after working, that I had managed people – said they were glad they hadn't worked for me!)

Well, when we got to the doorway, even after all the pushing and shoving, I do declare that even Twiggy couldn't have squeezed through, let alone somebody in a wheelchair.

It was one of those typical single-storey, flat-roofed houses with an external staircase to gain access to the roof. I looked around and the other three were close behind. I pointed them in the direction of the stairs and like lambs they followed meekly behind Jim and myself. I started again excusing us as we barged our way to the foot of the stairs. It seemed to take an absolute age to get there, but when we did I 'ordered' the other three to get hold of one corner of the wheelchair each, and we made our way laboriously up the steep stairs. We had to stop halfway up, on a little landing, because we all needed to take a breather, and we thought that perhaps our previous employers were correct in saying that we were 'past our best' and that we, individually, ought to think about our own personal downsizing!

It was there, at the landing window, that I first saw and heard the carpenter-preacher. Never have I seen such authority and gentleness combined in one person. Everyone in the room was just hanging on to every word he said. His voice, his gestures were so charismatic and I could see he held every person enthralled as he talked about life and the way that it should be lived. I turned to the other four, and all of them were equally entranced as I was, gazing through the window, but I realised that it was no good stopping there. So we started upon the upper section of the stairs and eventually arrived with our precious load on the roof, puffing and panting once more. It was only then that Harry said, 'Right then, clever clogs, what are we going to do now?'

And suddenly the total irony of the situation struck me for the very first time. Here we were, four grown men with their precious wheelchair-bound friend, up on top of a roof, wanting to be down on the ground – it would have been funny if it hadn't been so apparently stupid!

Now I want to stress and I want you to know that I and none of the others are the kind of people who go around vandalising property. Oh yes, I will admit if you press me that I once did have five penalty points on my driving licence, but that is the absolute extent of my breaking the law! It occurred to me that the roof wasn't very strong and Harry, who had been employed as a roofing contractor ought to know about these things, so I said to him, 'What do you reckon it would take to make a hole in the roof?' I am not quite sure who was the most surprised, me at making the suggestion, or Harry having heard it. But I reasoned that we hadn't come this far to let a roof get in the way of us and our goal.

We were very careful – made a little hole at first, then made it a little bigger, made sure that all the material we dislodged was kept on our side of the ceiling. Then, when the hole was big enough, we looked down and everyone, it seemed, was looking up at us. It was at that point that my eyes met those of the preacher.

It's hard to explain the penetrating look of those eyes. Yes, there was authority there but that seemed to be totally secondary to this tremendous gentleness and empathy. The smile on his face said it all. Do you know, I do believe that he knew better than we did just how we were going to get Jim down to be beside him. We debated how we were going to do it. The hole wasn't big enough for the wheelchair, so we took our sweaters off and made a kind of makeshift sling and we lowered Jim down to the only vacant spot in the whole room. People were packed in like sardines, but somehow there was just this one spot right in front of him. I do declare that when Jesus said to Jim, 'Your sins are forgiven. You are healed, so get up and walk' he wasn't looking at Jim at all, he was looking at me and perhaps the others. And just as later Jim declared that in addition to the heady sensation of having control of his body once more, there was a total feeling of well-being, I felt exactly the same.

I told you at the beginning that it was an incredible day. Well, all I can say is that life has never been the same since, not only for Jim, but for every one of us. Call me daft if you like, but we all agree that we were in the very presence of God himself that day, and not only that, but that presence has stayed with us ever since. You see, it wasn't only Jim who was healed.

* * * *

> When Jesus saw *their* faith, he said to the paralytic, 'Son, your sins are forgiven.'
>
> Mark 2:5

Now the point of telling you this story is that I want to suggest to you that those of us within the Christian Church can, if we have sufficient faith, achieve a great act of global healing. This will not require any vandalism of property, but it does require the dismantling of part, a very important part, of the present unjust global financial system. Most of you will know of Jubilee 2000 and of its aim to cancel, in celebration of the 2000th anniversary of the Saviour of the world's birth, the unpayable debt of the poorest nations of this world. Many of you will have sent your postcards with pound coins attached to the Chancellor of the Exchequer, or have signed one of the petitions, or might have been to Birmingham when the G7 (now the G8) group was meeting, and prayed earnestly for the removal of this quite obscene exploitation of the 'have-nots' by the 'haves' of the global family.

The proceeds from this slender publication will be sent as a contribution towards Jubilee 2000, but it is within each and every one of us to have faith in our ability to really do something once and for all to remove this injustice. I want to suggest that the success of this campaign would be the most incredible act of universal healing, bringing the kind of wholeness to millions which is their God-given birthright. Your faith that it can be achieved can be their healing, and corporately we can relive the healing at Capernaum, this time on a global scale. I dare to suggest that it is a far more fitting monument as a birthday present to an eternally-generous, incarnate God than any Greenwich Millennium Dome.

The God of justice and friend of the poor challenges each one of us to get involved in dismantling the current international ugly structure of exploitation and greed. Have faith that together (God and us) it can be achieved.

A final prayer:

God of justice and power, give us grace to have faith in ourselves; not the blind optimism of believing we can do everything if we only make enough noise and work extra hard, but the deep belief that because you believe in us, we can begin to do the same.

You offer us a partnership in which love is central, grounded in your eternal love for us. You challenge us to express our response by first returning that love, and then living out in loving service your endless compassion and concern for each and every aspect of your creation.

Forgive us, Father, that for too long humankind has squandered its inheritance – prefering to rape and not reap, steal and not steward, plunder and not provide, fight and not forgive. Forgive us, and love us better – make us better.

May we in the strong faith of Christ, and in your enabling power, do all we can to ensure that the celebrations for the 2000th anniversary of your incarnation herald a new dawn reflecting your selfless concern for justice, peace, and fairness for all your children.
Amen.

Brian Thornton

CONTRIBUTORS

Rev Dr Martyn Atkins spent ten years in circuit appointments, and then became School Chaplain and Head of Religious Studies in a Methodist residential school. He is currently Postgraduate Tutor in Evangelism, Missiology and Apologetics at Cliff College.

Caro Ayres is the Development Education Officer with the Methodist Relief and Development Fund. After attaining a degree in Oriental Studies she taught in the Palestinian territories for two years. This led to an MA in peace studies and her employment at MRDF.

Rev Mary Bailey has served in a number of circuits, including Daventry, where she was a part-time Prison Chaplain, and Great Yarmouth, where she developed a Direct Access Hostel. She was Superintendent of the Dome Mission, Brighton, and is currently Superintendent of the Brighton and Hove circuit.

Rev Stuart Burgess is currently the President of the Methodist Conference. He is Chairman of the York and Hull District, and the former Chaplain of the Universities of Nottingham and Birmingham.

Rev John Clarke worked in Kenya with the Methodist Missionary Society, and on returning to the UK he served as Superintendent in the Leominster and Ormskirk circuits. He became part of the Home Mission Division in the Leamington Spa Circuit, based at the Arthur Rank Centre. He became Director of the Centre in 1988 and retires from this post in 1999.

Rev Heather Cooper worked for an international bank before candidating for the ministry. She spent a year in Sheffield as a lay worker before training at Queens College, Birmingham. Her first appointment was in central Scotland, and she is now based in Warrington.

Rev Andrew Foster trained for the ministry at Hartley Victoria College, Manchester, and has served in Newcastle Brunswick, York South and York North circuits, in suburban and village churches. His current responsibilities include that of Hospital Chaplain and Chairman of Governors for an Anglican/Methodist day school.

Rev Michael Hayman retired in 1998 after 40 years in the ministry. He has served in eight appointments, spending the last 23 years in the North East London District, where he was Synod Secretary for five years.

Rev Albert Jewell became Pastoral Director of Methodist Homes in 1994 after 32 years' ministerial service in a wide variety of appointments. He has been instrumental in establishing a centre for the spirituality of ageing in Leeds. He serves as Administrator of the Sir Halley Stewart Age Awareness Project and Editor of the resources produced.

Rev Eddie Lacy served in the RAF before entering Headingly College to train for the Methodist ministry. He served in rural, urban mission and city centre circuits for 27 years before being appointed Chairman of the Oxford and Leicester District.

Rev John Lampard has served in four inner-city circuits in Leeds and London. He has been Superintendent of the South London Mission circuit since 1994. Previously he was Connexional Local Preachers' Secretary from 1985-94. He is also engaged in a doctoral research programme in the field of liturgy.

Rev Bill Lynn is Pastoral Director of NCH Action For Children and a member of the Senior Management Group at Highbury. A primary responsibility of his role concerns the relationship between the charity and the Methodist Church. Prior to joining NCH Action For Children he was a circuit minister in the Liverpool District.

Rev Steve Mann is a minister in Northampton-shire. Before entering the ministry he was a Chartered Accountant, specialising in trust and charity law. He also served as a lay worker in the East End of London and on Dartmoor.

Rev Dr Kathleen Richardson (Baroness Richardson of Calow) at the time of publication, is Co-ordinating Secretary for Interchurch and Other Relationships in the Methodist Church, retiring from this role in September 1999. She is a past President of the Methodist Conference, former Moderator of the Free Churches' Council, and one of the Presidents of Churches Together in England. In 1998 she was given a Life Peerage.

Brian Thornton is Vice-President of the Methodist Conference, and Chief Executive of the Methodist Publishing House. A local preacher, he is a Trustee of Wesley House, Cambridge, and Secretary of the International Publishing Committee of the World Methodist Council.

Rev Margaret Woodlock-Smith taught Religious Education at secondary level for a number of years in Kingston-upon-Hull. Her Christian background is Methodist and Salvation Army. Tadcaster is her third circuit appointment, and her first as a Superintendent minister.